100

THINGS TO DO IN
TOLEDO
BEFORE YOU
DIE

Photo courtesy of Destination Toledo

100
THINGS TO DO IN
TOLEDO
BEFORE YOU
DIE

· ·

TEDD LONG

REEDY PRESS

Copyright © 2021 by Reedy Press, LLC
Reedy Press
PO Box 5131
St. Louis, MO 63139, USA
www.reedypress.com

Library of Congress Control Number: 2020922406

ISBN: 9781681063003

Design by Jill Halpin

Photos by author unless otherwise noted.

Printed in the United States of America
21 22 23 24 25   5 4 3 2 1

DEDICATION

This book is gratefully dedicated to:

My family, for putting up with me when I start sentences with, "I'll bet you didn't know that . . ."

Bob Loeb, for impressing on me how important it is to "get to know your city" and for warmly demonstrating how lucky my family was to stumble into the loving arms of the Glass City.

CONTENTS

• •

Music and Entertainment

• •

• •

• •

• •

Photo courtesy of Destination Toledo

ACKNOWLEDGMENTS

This book was researched and transcribed with appreciation and gratitude to:

Lance Woodworth and the brilliant team at Destination Toledo for their tireless work in telling the Toledo story.

The hard-working team at Downtown Toledo for keeping the energy and vibrance of our downtown alive and well.

PREFACE

Way back in 1913, local business leaders in Toledo asked area residents to suggest a catchphrase that described how they feel about life in Toledo. From 7,000 entries, the winning phrase—You Will Do Better in Toledo—still resonates more than 100 years later. In fact, every December 16th, nearly 300,000 Toledo-area residents celebrate "You Will Do Better in Toledo Day" to take their hats off to the Glass City and show their pride in living in a vibrant and welcoming community.

The best of both worlds is on offer in the Toledo region: a sophisticated city with a small town vibe, surrounded by first-class parks, Maumee Bay and Lake Erie, and a mix of unique suburban and rural communities offering something to do 365 days of the year. Toledo brings a lot to the table, no matter what piques your interest, including first-class sports and outdoor recreation, world-class museums, exciting nightlife, and award-winning restaurants and theatre. And, when you want to explore beyond the city, many outstanding recreation destinations—from lakes, bays, and rivers to the world's most incredible amusement park—are just a short drive away.

I'm proud of my city, and I love sharing the Toledo story with others. We've come a long way in the 30-plus years since my wife and I arrived here from the Chicago suburbs. There is now a noticeable feeling of satisfaction and pride by Toledoans in how their city has shed its rust-belt image by embracing creativity and new technology. Alan Solomon of the *Chicago Tribune* described it best in a review entitled, "Holy Toledo! Ohio's 'Glass City' Is Worth a Trip" when he closed his appraisal with this spot-on observation: "There's a homegrown swagger here that's, well, wholly Toledo."

My hope is that whether you are a lifelong Toledoan or just here for a visit, after exploring the things to do in this book, you too will feel that wholly Toledo pride.

—Tedd Long

PACKO'S at the Park

7 SOUTH SUPERIOR

Photo courtesy of Destination Toledo

FOOD AND DRINK

DELIGHT IN
A WORLD-FAMOUS HUNGARIAN HOT DOG AT TONY PACKO'S

No trip to Toledo would be complete without a stop at the legendary Tony Packo's, made famous by Toledo's own Jamie Farr, who played Corporal Klinger on the hit TV show *M*A*S*H*. The son of Hungarian immigrants, Tony Packo was a native of Toledo's East Side neighborhood known as Birmingham. In 1932, during the height of the Great Depression, 24-year-old Tony and his wife, Rose, borrowed $100 from family members to open a small sandwich and ice cream shop. Looking to add something special to his menu, Packo decided to add his homemade spicy chili sauce to give a little zing to the flavor of his hot dogs. He also used a Hungarian sausage called Kolbász that was large enough to split in half lengthwise and still ask the customary 5 cents that other restaurants charged for a full-sized hot dog.

By 1935, Tony and Rose were able to buy an East Side building of their own. They purchased a wedge-shaped shop at Front and Consaul Streets, and Packo's has been there ever since! In late June 1972, Burt Reynolds stopped by Packo's to enjoy a meal after a local performance. When asked for his autograph, Reynolds flippantly picked up a hot dog bun, signed it, and the tradition of celebrity "bun signing" at Packo's was born.

1902 Front St., (419) 691-6054

TIP

While there are numerous Packo eateries located in the Toledo area, you must make a visit to the original East Side restaurant to fully enjoy the Packo history and ambiance. Enjoy lunch or dinner while browsing the celebrity-signed hot dog buns displayed on the café walls. Along with the world-famous hot dog, other Hungarian specialties include chicken paprikash, stuffed cabbage, apple strudel, dumplings, and their newest sensation, fried green pickles. Free and convenient parking is right across the street.

SAVOR PACZKI
FROM BAKERY UNLIMITED

Bakery Unlimited was established in 1989 by owner Scott Nugent, a third-generation baker. His baking career began with washing pans and bowls at age 6. By the age of 13, he was decorating wedding cakes and practicing the baking lessons and family recipes his legendary father, Dave Nugent, had passed on to him. His delicious, homemade baked goods, from doughnuts to cream puffs, specialty cakes to specialty pies, begin at Bakery Unlimited. Some of their signature baked goods include eclairs, cakes, pies, and more. They also feature seasonal items for all holidays, including their world-famous, homemade paczki.

So what's paczki, you may ask? Paczki (pronounced POONCH-key, that's the plural, and the singular is paczek, pronounced POONCH-ek) are plump, doughnut-like pastries. Polish people from Toledo will tell you that in their tradition, these delicacies are baked to use up the butter, eggs, milk, and other rich foods that are supposed to be shunned during the penitential period of Lent. Here in the Glass City, Fat Tuesday, or Paczki Day, is a date of feasting before the fast that comes with Ash Wednesday. If you are in town for Fat Tuesday, get yourself a sack of paczki.

4427 Secor Rd., (419) 472-7098, bakeryunlimitedtoledo.com

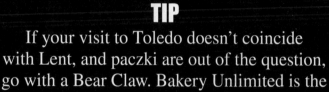

TIP

If your visit to Toledo doesn't coincide with Lent, and paczki are out of the question, go with a Bear Claw. Bakery Unlimited is the last bakery to make Hinkle's famous Bear Claws, a Toledo tradition since 1961.

SHOP FOR OLD WORLD KIELBASA
AT STANLEY'S MARKET

Toledo is home to a thriving Polish community that has been an integral part of our city's culture for generations. The Polish provide so much flavor to the Glass City, and nowhere is their enduring legacy of delicious food and friendly spirit more evident than at Stanley's!

Stanley's Market has stood at 3302 Stickney Avenue in the Lagrinka Polish neighborhood since the 1930s when the original Mr. Stanley—Stanley Goscin—founded the business. The Zychowicz family picked up the tradition in 1955. Today, Stanley's Market stands little changed from its beginning as a quality neighborhood grocery store and fine meats market.

When I visit Stanley's, I always go in intending to buy a few pounds of their delicious kielbasa, but I always walk out with much more. They carry a full line of unique-to-Toledo Polish items, including homemade delicacies such as kapusta (sweet and sour cabbage), pierogi (filled dumplings), czarnina (traditional sweet soup), bigos (Polish hunters stew), placek (Polish coffee cake), and golabki (stuffed cabbage rolls). I also enjoy their salads, fresh-baked loaves of bread, and lunch meats. Stanley's is also the go-to place for Polish gift items.

3302 Stickney Ave., (419) 726-4347
stanleysmarketstore.com

TAKE HOME KOLBÁSZ AND HURKA
FROM TAKACS GROCERY & MEATS

When you visit Toledo, and you want a quality sausage, you have to consider the geography. If you want kielbasa, head to the north end and visit Stanley's in the Polish Village. If you're looking for a kolbász, you head over to Takacs in East Toledo's Birmingham neighborhood—Toledo's Hungarian enclave named after Birmingham, England, in the early 1900s because it resembled the busy steel town.

Takacs butcher shop has been around for more than 50 years and has excellent Hungarian specialties. The kolbász here is the best in town, and their natural skin hot dogs are the bomb, as is everything else they put their hand to at Takacs. It's not easy to find, but if you are visiting the original Packo's, the world-famous hot dog emporium located at Front and Consaul, you're not too far from Takacs. Just drive down Consaul, hang a left at Genesee, and look for a market that's been there since God was in short pants. It's not hard to miss.

Walk in (if they're open) and order several pounds of whatever tickles your nose. The prices are reasonable, and they have a following. If you happen to be from out of town, make sure to stock up because I guarantee you won't find choice foodstuff like this anywhere else.

1956 Genesee St., (419) 693-9233

TAME A GARBAGE SALAD
AT GRUMPY'S

Grumpy's is a uniquely Toledo gem serving breakfast, sandwiches, and homemade desserts in a cozy, brick-walled space on Huron Street in Toledo's Warehouse District.

Besides being known for outstanding scratch-made delicacies, Grumpy's is also known for its remarkable backstory. The restaurant's roots were planted about 30 years ago when Horn Hardware, a family-run shop located at Broadway and Western Avenue, began selling lunch meat and cheese out of a cooler to carpenters, contractors, and other hardware buyers. As the story goes, customers began requesting bread to go along with their meats and cheese, and the Horns soon found themselves offering sandwiches along with nails, paint, and hand tools. As the demand for sandwiches grew, the Horn's lunch counter evolved to accommodate it. Eventually, they opened up Grumpy's at Michigan and Washington Streets and then moved to their current home on Huron Street. Today, the restaurant is still run by members of the Horn family.

While Grumpy's menu may have its roots in hardware store sandwiches, their tasty burgers, soups, and sandwiches are unlike any you'll find anywhere else. If you are looking for something greener, Grumpy's Garbage Salad is a local favorite. It's a mixed greens salad with onions, tomatoes, mushrooms, grilled chicken, raisins, and four kinds of cheese (provolone, mozzarella, feta, and fresh parmesan)—tossed together with their award-winning poppy seed dressing and topped off with homemade croutons and bacon. The salad's salty-sweet flavor is truly delicious. The *Toledo Free Press* describes it as "a carnival of different tastes and textures."

While you're there, don't forget to take home a bottle of their salad dressing to share with friends and family.

34 S Huron St., (419) 241-6728, grumpys.net

UPGRADE YOUR WEEKEND
WITH SUNDAY BRUNCH AT
MANHATTAN'S PUB AND CHEER

Toledo's Uptown District, located between downtown Toledo and the Old West End neighborhood, is known for its funky shops and restaurants and Toledo's homegrown artistic renaissance. Manhattan's sits in the heart of Uptown on Adams Street and helps amplify the neighborhood's vibrance and energy.

Featuring American fare with a New York–inspired menu, in a warm, brick-walled setting lovingly restored by the Lahey's back in 2002, Manhattan's is known for great food, top-notch live entertainment, and a terrific patio for outside dining. With that said, this friendly spot may be best known for its delectable Sunday Brunch. This delicious buffet offers a sundry of breakfast choices and includes a free mimosa! It's a terrific way to start your Sunday morning any time of the year.

1516 Adams St., (419) 243-6675
manhattanstoledo.com

Are you in downtown Toledo looking for a bite to eat? There's a great variety of excellent choices. Here's a small sampling of local favorites to try:

Balance Pan-Asian Grille
Asian-Fusion.
215 N Summit St.
(419) 243-2222, balancegrille.com

Original Sub Shop and Deli
Sub shop with homemade soups and
lots of friendly faces.
401 Broadway St.
(419) 243-4857, originalsub.com

The Real Seafood Company
Featuring fresh seafood and the most spectacular
view of downtown Toledo.
22 Main St. (The Docks)
(888) 456-3463, realseafoodcotoledo.com

Coney Island Restaurant
Greek diner—the oldest restaurant in Toledo!
430 N Superior St.
(419) 244-8050
facebook.com/ConeyIslandDowntownToledo

Fowl & Fodder
Excellent farm to table fare.
614 Adams St.
(419) 214-1588, fodderrestaurants.com

REVEL IN AFRICAN AMERICAN CUISINE
AT JOSEPHINE'S KITCHEN

Josephine's Kitchen is a low-key, no-frills shop offering classic soul food and comfort dishes such as shrimp, meatloaf, mac & cheese, roast turkey, fried chicken, catfish, greens, and Sunday dinners with all the fixings. Since it's a pretty simple place: small, clean, sparse—not big on presentation or décor—you might think of it as Toledo's "soul food" carryout.

Regardless of the dimensions or humble atmosphere, Josephine's is big on personality and flavor. The food is the epitome of authentic soul food, and the staff takes great pride in treating their customers as extended family. Simply put, this is grandma's southern cooking—heavy, savory, flavorful, and big on the love.

902 Lagrange St., (419) 242-6666

CELEBRATE CHILI MAC
AT IDEAL HOT DOG

They say that chili mac originated in Cincinnati when a couple of Macedonian immigrants began serving chili over noodles at their small burlesque theatre in the 1920s. One hundred years later, chili mac or "Cincinnati Chili" has become a unique regional dish. Here in northwest Ohio, when people debate where to experience the best local chili mac, some say, "If it ain't Ideal, it ain't real chili mac!"

Ideal Hot Dog is a legendary Toledo greasy spoon (that's a complimentary term) with two locations, north and south of downtown. While Ideal offers a wide variety of tasty, filling meals at a fair price, it's the chili mac that most folks order, and I highly recommend you do the same. Your chili mac experience at Ideal begins with a large steaming portion of spaghetti pasta, topped first with your preference of beans and/or onions, then covered with their famous secretly spiced chili mac sauce made fresh daily, and topped off with a mountain of shredded cheddar (or Romano) cheese. Add two slices of garlic bread, and you're off to chili mac nirvana! You'll enjoy hints of cumin and paprika in the blended sauce, which goes perfectly with the piping hot pasta, onions, and beans. Don't hold back here—get the jumbo plate and don't forget the cheese!

1135 W Alexis Rd.
or 4330 Heatherdowns Blvd., (419) 478-3023

DRINK IN SOME TOLEDO HISTORY
AT MAUMEE BAY BREWERY

More than 150 years ago, Isaiah Rogers, the architect of the Maxwell House Hotel in Nashville, the Ohio Statehouse in Columbus, and the John Jacob Astor House in New York, was commissioned by Major William Oliver to design the Oliver House along the Maumee River on Toledo's Middlegrounds. Up to that time, hotel accommodations in Toledo were mostly of the country inn variety, but the Oliver House was a luxury hotel with parlors, damask wall fabrics, a rosewood piano, and excellent cuisine served in the most "exotic" style. Today, the Oliver House is home to apartments, a few restaurants, and the Maumee Bay Brewery.

The Maumee Bay Brewery carries on a Toledo beer legacy with on-site brewing of local favorite, Buckeye Beer, along with many other pleasing varieties of beer. Before you sit down to sip a pint of their Glasshopper IPA, made from Centennial hops, or enjoy a bite to eat, take a tour of the historic Oliver House. It once served as a convalescent center for soldiers wounded during the Spanish-American War, and some say this landmark building has a haunted reputation.

27 Broadway St., (419) 243-1302, mbaybrew.com

The Toledo area offers excellent choices
for hometown hops.

Black Frog Brewery
You have to try their Cream of the Frog crisp ale.
831 S McCord Rd., Holland, blackfrogbrewery.com

Ernest Brew
Taste the granola-inspired Crunchy Hippie.
4342 S Detroit Ave., earnestbrewworks.com

Inside the Five
Try the Boss Stout—it's brewed with oatmeal.
5703 Main St., Sylvania, insidethefivebrewing.com

Patron Saints Brewery
Nano brewery crafting a wide variety of Saintly beers.
4730 Bancroft St., facebook.com/patronsaintsbrewery

Pavlov's Brewing Company
Home of the conditioned response.
Try their Sitting Pretty IPA (ABV 8.5%).
7548 Lewis Ave., Temperance, MI, pavlovsbrew.com

Upside Brewing
Knock back a few pints of their 10 Mile Red Ale and
nosh on some J & G Pizza.
5692 Main St., Sylvania, facebook.com/
UpsideBrewing/

ENJOY AN EXQUISITE SEASONAL MENU
AT REGISTRY BISTRO

Uniquely located in a historic building that was once Toledo's premier hotel, Registry Bistro is a modern restaurant pairing eclectic New American dishes on small plates at reasonable prices—for the entire table to share—with wine, craft beer, and signature cocktails.

Chef Erika Rapp's education at the Culinary Institute of America, coupled with experience gained from her travel and exposure to a kaleidoscope of cuisines, has influenced her to create wonderfully diverse and artfully crafted modern American dishes that leverage the abundance of locally sourced produce and specialty items.

When asked about her cooking style, she says, "I am continually inspired by the change of seasons in northwest Ohio and the regional cuisines of America. I try to reflect both in the way I cook."

Because Erika's menu is seasonal, it's hard for me to recommend a favorite dish, but I recommend you freestyle and try something new. You won't be disappointed.

144 N Superior St., (419) 725-0444, registrybistro.com

"STEAK" YOUR CLAIM
FOR FAMILY TRADITION AT MANCY'S

Toledo has always been a steak town. Sure, we're known for our fresh Lake Erie walleye and perch, but chances are, when most folks look back on a great meal in the Glass City, it usually includes a slab of beef. Toledoans love their steakhouses.

Mancy's is the most iconic steakhouse in Toledo. It's the perfect place for experiencing all the things people love about an unrushed elegant dining experience: fantastic steaks, great sides, and attentive, friendly service. The ambiance is a throwback but in a charming way. Even though it's consistently rated as one of the top fine dining restaurants in the area, it isn't fancy or stuffy. The crowd is a mixed bag of regulars, visitors, and locals celebrating birthdays or anniversaries, so no matter your occasion, this is the right choice. "Steak" your claim and celebrate.

953 Phillips Ave., (419) 476-4154, mancys.com

RELISH A SLICE OF TOLEDO
AT INKY'S

When anyone asks me if there are any old-school Italian joints left in Toledo, I instantly mention Inky's. Owned and operated by the Incorvaia family for three generations, this heirloom restaurant features homemade Italian cuisine served in a family atmosphere. Whether it's lunch or dinner, dine in or carry out, Inky's has been dishing up pizza pies, lasagna, pasta, steak, and seafood for more than 60 years.

Make sure you tuck a napkin into your collar as you lap up Inky's somewhat sweet and addictive signature red sauce. It complements everything from their delicious chicken parm to their thin-crust pizza. My go-to lunch at Inky's is a small pepperoni pizza coupled with their midget salad and house dressing. Give it a try!

3945 N Detroit Ave., (419) 476-0500, inkysitalianfoods.com

MAKE A CHILI DOG PILGRIMAGE
TO RUDY'S

When president Barak Obama visited the Glass City in 2011, he didn't have to search far for a taste of Toledo. He and his entourage elected Rudy's on Sylvania Avenue as the place to go. This family-owned chain of six eateries was launched by Rudy Poturedes (Uncle Rudy) back in 1920 as a single hot dog stand. In due course, Uncle Rudy opened a full-fledged restaurant in the 1930s. After Uncle Rudy passed away in 1960, the Dionyssiou brothers, Harry and Andreas took over and later, in 1971, moved the restaurant to its current location on Sylvania Avenue.

Not sure what to order? You can't go wrong with former president Obama's selection: two chili dogs with onions, mustard, and cheese; French fries; and a bowl of chili. By the way, the then president also bought meals for Sen. Sherrod Brown, Rep. Marcy Kaptur, and Mayor Mike Bell, who accompanied him on his stop at Rudy's. Mike Bell convinced the then commander in chief to wash his meal down with a Faygo red pop. Try it!

946 W Sylvania Ave., (419) 478-7095, rudyshotdog.com

LAVISH YOUR SOUL WITH A VIEW
FROM THE HEIGHTS

We all know that cocktails taste better when paired with a spectacular view. I don't have a lot to say about why The Heights is THE place for a panoramic view and a refreshing drink because there is no place like it anywhere else in northwest Ohio. Day or night, indoors or outside, The Heights towers over downtown Toledo with its positive vibes, sleek industrial décor, extensive menu, and, of course, breathtaking views.

Located on top of the Renaissance Hotel, this stylish, one-of-a-kind rooftop bar offers hand-crafted cocktails, award-winning craft beers, global bites, bird's-eye views of the mighty Maumee River, Lake Erie's Maumee Bay, and the impressive Toledo skyline. I'm a big fan of their small plates and wood-fired pizzas! Simply put, if you want to enjoy a great view of the Glass City, get there!

444 N Summit St., (419) 243-7565, theheightstoledo.com

DRINK IN GLASS CITY VIBES
AT TOLEDO SPIRITS'
BELLWETHER COCKTAIL BAR

Bellwether at Toledo Spirits is a cocktail bar and kitchen created to showcase Toledo's favorite distiller's spirits in exciting, inventive cocktails. This bar is a very hip place to spend an evening. The relaxed atmosphere is perfect for date night, business meetings, private events, or group get-togethers.

The staff are top-notch professionals and know their business well. So, explore a little! Go out on a limb and try something new at Bellwether. You won't regret it.

1301 N Summit St., (419) 662-9521, toledospirits.com

MEET YOUR FRIENDS
AT NICK & JIMMY'S

This busy neighborhood bar located across the street from the Franklin Park Mall starts the day serving breakfast and is open late into the night hosting the bar crowd. If there was ever a real-life model for all the friendly bars seen on television over the years, Nick & Jimmy's is it. Opened in 1979 with a New Orleans theme, this West Toledo pub offers typical American roadhouse food, table games, pool tables, and plenty of big-screen TVs for all the sports action.

Don't miss the weekend live music on the patio in the summer.

4956 Monroe St., (419) 472-0756, nickandjimmys.com

FEAST ON GREEK DELICACIES
AT MANO'S GREEK RESTAURANT

This brick-walled eatery with a traditional Mediterranean menu, including moussaka, gyros, and saganaki, has been Toledo's go-to restaurant for authentic Greek cuisine for more than 30 years. Located in the Uptown District at 17th and Adams Streets, Manos offers lunch and dinner in a comfortable, casual, and relaxing atmosphere.

Are you looking for something different? Try any of their famous salads, affectionately named after some of their favorite customers. Me? I'm all about the Howard Rosenbaum salad. Make sure you're hungry—Howard's salad is a meal!

1701 Adams St., (419) 244-4479, manosgreekrestaurant.com

TIP

The Uptown District is a celebration of Toledo's dynamic culture and community. Two great places to soak in the Uptown neighborhood vibe is the Ottawa Tavern or Wesley's Bar & Grill. The perfect place to end a night out in Uptown is The Attic, located above Mano's. Are you visiting at Halloween time? Don't forget the annual Adams Street Zombie Crawl, where 20,000 zombies take over the Uptown neighborhood.

Check this out! Uptown has the special recognition of having been designated as one of Ohio's first outdoor refreshment areas. Residents and visitors alike can socialize outdoors along Adams Street with alcoholic beverages from participating bars.

FANCY AN EXTRAORDINARY DINING EXPERIENCE
AT GEORGIO'S CAFÉ INTERNATIONAL

Every downtown has that one place where you're bound to run into the city's heavy hitters—Georgio's is that place in Toledo, and why not? This high-end, enduring eatery is known for its elegant lunches and memorable dinners. Brothers Chris and George Kamilaris feature the freshest seafood, succulent steaks and chops, and delicious pasta dishes enhanced by the perfect bottle of wine. Georgio's intimate atmosphere conveys a relaxed elegance, and their friendly and knowledgeable staff ensure your complete satisfaction.

The Zagat Survey recognized Georgio's as a "delight in every way." While I recommend you ask for a menu, don't be afraid to simply ask your server what fresh items chefs Chris or George recommend from the kitchen and go for it. Bon appétit!

426 N Superior St., (419) 242-2424, georgiostoledo.com

EXPERIENCE TOLEDO'S FINEST TORTELLINI
AT M OSTERIA & BAR

With a cuisine featuring a combination of traditional Italian classics, artisan pizzas, and state-of-the-art fare, M Osteria & Bar will meet the needs of the choosiest fine Italian dining connoisseur. All the offerings are prepared with an emphasis on using only the freshest, prime ingredients, keeping the integrity of traditional dishes while incorporating style and flare. My go-to favorite is their brisket tortellini, made from a five-hour braised brisket, plus house-made tortellini and ricotta. Così Buono!

M Osteria also offers an impressive wine list, extensive signature drinks, and an ellent craft beer selection. Dessert? Well. M Oster eats homemade from the fine m monthly to reflect their

222, mosteriatoledo.com

FUEL YOUR BODY
AND YOUR HEART
AT MICHAEL'S BAR AND GRILL

Family owned and operated since 1922, Michael's is a warm and cozy, old-school diner serving excellent homemade soups, salads, and daily specials at the best prices in town. When I say "old school," I mean it. Walking into this place is like a step back in time and not just because of the great Toledo memorabilia hanging on the walls. The Yakumithis family and their staff go out of their way to wrap their arms around you and make you feel at home. You can dine in at their lunch counter, cozy up in a booth, enjoy their private group meeting room, or hang out on their outdoor patio. While the food and atmosphere are outstanding, don't forget the full-service bar!

Make sure you say hello to George behind the counter; he's a wonder to watch work the grill when the place is busy. He may be the best short-order cook in Toledo—and the friendliest too!

901 Monroe St., (419) 241-3900, michaelsbarandgrill.com

EAT VEGAN
IN THE GLASS CITY

Over the past 10 years, the Toledo area has seen several locally owned restaurants offer tasty vegan dishes as part of their standard fare. We even have an online resource for vegans or anyone curious about healthy eating at www.vegantoledo.com.

Vegan Toledo, vegantoledo.com

If you are searching for that perfect vegan dish,
here are a few places to consider:

The Leaf and Seed Café & Food Truck
Dedicated to using locally sourced, non-GMO organic products.
10th St., theleafandseed.com

Frankly Plant Based Kitchen Food Truck
Known for their plant-based hot dogs.
Various locations, franklypbk.com

Tiger Bakery & Deli
Also a fantastic place for some of the freshest
Mediterranean food in town.
4215 Monroe St. and 6710 W Central Ave., Sylvania, tigerbakery.com

Rice Blvd
An excellent little spot specializing in sushi,
bento box, and rice bowls.
1440 Secor Rd., riceblvd.com

Ameera Mediterranean Bistro
A terrific place serving lots of vegan options in a warm
and friendly atmosphere.
5217 Main St., Sylvania, ameeramediterraneanbistro.com

SAMPLE HOMEMADE SWEETNESS
FROM WIXEY BAKERY

Wixey Bakery has been a part of Toledo history for more than 80 years, and, thankfully, while times have changed, Wixey Bakery hasn't. Today, fourth-generation family members, Brian Wixey and Denise Wixey-Coulter can be found at the bakery working side by side with their father, Dennis Wixey. They still use the family's original recipes and classic baking approaches to provide Toledo with their perfect wedding and birthday cakes and their made-from-scratch bakery items.

Tucked inside a colorful neighborhood south of the Toledo Zoo, this place has always been family owned and operated. While known for their fresh cakes, doughnuts, pastries, and frosted sugar cookies, don't miss their salsa!

2017 Glendale Ave., (419) 382-6684, wixeysbakery.com

DIG INTO AUTHENTIC MEXICAN FRESHNESS
AT SAN MARCOS TAQUERIA & GROCERY

Years ago, the Toledo lunch crowd gladly lined up in long queues to buy fresh-made tacos from the meat counter at San Marcos grocery store. Today, a full service, no-frills taqueria serves simple, traditional Mexican dishes in a style that is all its own.

Their tacos are simply superb. I suggest you go with the Supremo with steak, lettuce, onion, tomato, avocado, cheese, and sour cream. With just the right amount of fresh cilantro, add a squeeze of fresh lime, and you are in taco heaven. There is no place like it in Toledo. Located off the High-Level Bridge's west ramp, San Marcos is the go-to place for authentic Mexican food and grocery products. Oh, I almost forgot, don't forget to sample a refreshing margarita on their patio!

235 Broadway St., (419) 244-2373, sanmarcosmexicanrestaurants.com

GET A FEEL FOR THE EAST SIDE
AT MICHAEL'S CAFÉ & BAKERY

When you cross the Martin Luther King Bridge to head over to the East Side from downtown Toledo, the building up ahead anchoring the northeast corner of Front and Main dominates your view. This old landmark is the Weber Block. Inside you'll find Michael's, a tranquil bakery and café renowned for their homemade pastries, soups, and sandwiches. For me, Michael's is the queen of Toledo comfort food. When I stop by, I always end up pausing halfway through my meal to savor the contentment and nostalgia that comes with food that tastes like my Grandma made it.

Michael's is within walking distance of Toledo's new Glass City Metropark, so don't be shy about grabbing your meal to go and enjoying a riverfront view of the city while you enjoy some comfort food.

101 Main St., (419) 698-2988, michaelsoftoledo.com

WASH DOWN A FLAMING MOE
AT MOE'S PLACE

When people ask me to rank the best hamburgers in our area, Moe's is always at the top of my list. Don't let the humble looks of this "shot and a beer" bar stop you from stopping in for a bite to eat. Order whatever you want—the menu is a mile long, and it's all good. I highly recommend the Flaming Moe; this half-pound burger is one of the best in town. Not a burger fan? Try the Big Bird, a deep-fried chicken breast dipped in your choice of sauce, served on ciabatta bread.

620 Dixie Highway, Rossford, (419) 666-9314
moesplacerossford.com

MUSIC AND ENTERTAINMENT

APPEASE
YOUR TASTE BUDS
AND YOUR EARS
AT YE OLDE DURTY BIRD

If you're looking to add some live music with your burger craving, this traditional tavern, housed in the Grand Hotel building built in 1867, is the best bet. Ye Olde Durty Bird, Toledo's original gastropub, offers a wide-ranging menu of great food and pints of cold beer with free live music. It's right across the street from Fifth Third Field, home of the Toledo Mud Hens. Pregame or postgame, lunch or dinner, the Durty Bird captures the Glass City's local flavor and offers an entertaining approach to casual dining!

2 S St. Clair St., (419) 243-2473, yeoldedurtybird.com

TIP
No trip to the Durty Bird is complete without sampling a few of their incredible chicken wings slathered in the pub's signature "Durty" sauce.

BELLY UP TO THE BAR
AT SODBUSTER'S

Back when Sylvania was a one-stoplight town, the Sodbuster Bar opened as a neighborhood hangout. Today it's still that, but with a little something for everyone. Voted Sylvania's best bar and proud of it, Sodbusters features good food and great live music every weekend from September to May.

Try a burger or one of their tasty pizzas. They have lots of toppings to choose from and ALWAYS have the game on one of their TVs.

5758 Main St., Sylvania, (419) 517-1045, sodbusterbar.com

LOOSEN UP
AT COCK & BULL

Born out of the owner's love for local music and craft beer, the Cock n' Bull is located in the historic Warehouse District, just steps away from Fifth Third Field and the Huntington Center. This lively, family-friendly sports bar and American eatery features craft beer, acoustic sets during the week, and local rock bands on the weekends. While live music is key to Cock n' Bull's charm, don't forget the craft beers. This place is known for offering 34 beers on tap that change every few days, and management will tell you that patrons will come in just to see what's new.

If great music and an incredible selection of craft beers aren't enough for you, try the food. I'm a massive fan of their slow-roasted chicken. After six hours of roasting, the succulent bird is fall-off-the-bone tender and melts in your mouth!

Enjoy your visit inside or out—they have a comfortable covered patio.

9 N Huron St., (419) 244-2855, cocknbulltoledo.com

TOLEDO'S WAREHOUSE DISTRICT

You'll see Toledo's Warehouse District pop up quite often in this list. That's because this historic neighborhood packs big city vibes into a few city blocks. The Warehouse District is alive with the buzz of commerce during the day, and once the workday ends, more than 20 pubs and restaurants fill up thanks to a vibrant nightlife. This eclectic zone takes full advantage of the excellent food, convenient walkability, unique residential living spaces, major sports stadiums, and concert venues packed inside its boundaries.

As Toledo blossomed in the latter half of the 1800s, the Warehouse District grew up around Swan Creek and its easy access to the Maumee River and Lake Erie to become a regional center for warehousing and manufacturing. It was also home of the notorious Tenderloin, Toledo's infamous red-light district. But that's all in the past. Today, the revitalized Warehouse District is a perfect blend of retail business, residential living, and commercial enterprise where people live, work, and play.

BINGE ON MUSIC AND PIZZA
AT THE VILLAGE IDIOT

Located in beautiful Uptown Maumee, The Village Idiot stands out on its own in the Toledo-area bar scene. Along with being voted Toledo's Best Pizza and Best Local Venue, they host live music 365 days a year. Yep, they've been open every single day for the past 15 years! They host some of the best national acts who play only here, such as Dale Watson, The Day Drinkers, Luke Winslow-King, The War & Treaty, Radio Free Honduras, Shawn James, and countless others, as well as the best local talent around. Whether you stop by for a show or just enjoy an afternoon of pizza and an incredible selection of craft beer, you'll soon see why only an idiot would miss out on this local gem.

309 Conant St., Maumee, (419) 893-7281, villageidiotmaumee.com

DIG THE GIG GUIDE
AT TOLEDO.COM OR CHART YOUR EXPLORATION AT DESTINATION TOLEDO

Toledo.com's Gig Guide is Toledo's most up-to-date list of area music venues and their live performance schedules. Stay updated on local concerts and shows featuring local, regional, and national acts of all genres at Toledo.com.

If you want to chart a deeper dive into Toledo beyond the bucket list contained in this book, look no further than Destination Toledo—the area's official Destination Marketing Organization. They provide extraordinary resources for visitors, including all the latest information on events, conferences, and lodging. Their annual Destination Guide is an excellent road map for enjoying the most fun during your visit to Toledo.

toledo.com/gig-guide, visittoledo.org

SUPPORT THE ARTS
AT THE VALENTINE THEATRE

The Valentine Theatre graces the corner of Superior and Adams Streets. The 901-seat Victorian-era facility, operated by the Toledo Cultural Arts Center, Inc., was opened in 1895 and presents a wide variety of entertainment, from symphony concerts and Broadway shows to ballet and dance programs. The Valentine is also a first-rate venue for special events.

After a $28 million renovation was unveiled on October 9, 1999, the theatre has hosted more than 50 community groups, including the Toledo Symphony, Toledo Opera, Toledo Ballet, Ballet Theatre of Toledo, Toledo Jazz Society, Masterworks Chorale, University of Toledo, area high schools, and many others. The notable building was added to the National Register of Historic Places on May 19, 1987.

410 Adams St., (419) 242-2787, valentinetheatre.com

DISCOVER CLASSICS
AT THE PERISTYLE

The Toledo Museum of Art's Peristyle is a charming 1,750-seat concert hall in the museum's east wing. Over the years, it has served as a principal concert space for the Toledo Symphony Orchestra and hosts the museum's Masters Series. Added in 1933 at the direction of Florence Scott Libbey, a founder and significant benefactor of the museum, the Peristyle was designed in a classical style to match the museum's exterior. Seating is divided into floor and riser sections, with the riser seating arranged in a half-circle, similar to a Greek theater. At the back of the riser seating, 28 Ionic columns give the concert hall its name. Lighting throughout the theatre, including the sky-colored, domed ceiling, creates the ambiance of an evening concert in an outdoor Greek garden.

Make sure you check the museum's events calendar; they often offer companion lectures and events to make your night out at the Peristyle a memorable and intellectually stimulating experience.

2445 Monroe St., (419) 255-8000, toledomuseum.org

EXPLORE THE WORLD OF MUSIC
WITH THE TOLEDO SYMPHONY

Toledo offers a few indisputably unique amenities that set it apart from other similar-sized cities in the Great Lakes region. One that stands out is our exceptional symphony. The Toledo Symphony Orchestra (or TSO) is home to regional professional musicians and teachers who deliver outstanding performances and music education throughout the year.

From a performance perspective, the TSO offers a wide variety of programming, including a charming chamber series set in intimate settings around the city, an enjoyable family series designed for all ages, and a contemporary pops series featuring musical favorites from today and yesterday. I guarantee the TSO's masterworks series will delight the most refined classical music enthusiast's sophisticated ear. Individual and group tickets for TSO programs are best purchased online or over the phone.

From an educational perspective, the Toledo Symphony School of Music provides high-quality, family-focused music instruction to students from throughout our region.

1838 Parkwood Ave., (419) 246-8000, toledosymphony.com

LET DANCE SOOTHE YOUR SOUL
WITH THE TOLEDO BALLET

The Toledo Ballet was founded in 1939 by Marie Bollinger Vogt. Throughout its history, this artistic group has been a leader in the regional performing arts community by cultivating the love of dance through education, performance, and outreach. While its name says "Ballet," Toledo Ballet also offers an extensive contemporary division, a conditioning division, and even musical theatre.

Toledo Ballet recently merged with the Toledo Symphony Orchestra to form the Toledo Alliance for the Performing Arts to inspire our region to come together through the performing arts. Today, these two organizations, sharing 160 years of history, offer audiences diverse and outstanding performances from September to May.

5327 Monroe St., (419) 471-0049, toledoballet.com

ADORE MUSIC UNDER THE STARS
AT THE TOLEDO ZOO AMPHITHEATER

While the Toledo Zoo has been ranked #1 nationally by *USA Today* in a Readers' Choice of favorite zoos, it's also a fantastic place to enjoy top musical and comedic performances by world-renowned acts during its annual summer-season concerts. The beautiful Zoo Amphitheater is one of our area's best outdoor venues with seats close to the stage where you can enjoy an intimate show with legends such as Bob Dylan, Paul Simon, or Buddy Guy, to name a few. Besides the top-notch entertainment, there are tasty libations!

Built by the WPA and dedicated in 1936, the Zoo Amphitheater is also the home of Music Under the Stars, which is a free concert series highlighting community bands that dates back to the 1950s. Check out the zoo's website for the latest information on concerts and the Music Under the Stars lineup. Attending a performance at the Zoo Amphitheater is a blast, but make sure you arrive early enough to allow time to park and enjoy the stroll to your seats from the zoo's Anthony Wayne Trail entrance.

2 Hippo Way, (419) 385-5721, toledozoo.org/concerts

TIP

I refer to the WPA in quite a few of the descriptions on this list. WPA stands for Works Progress Administration. Since Toledo was hit incredibly hard with widespread unemployment during the Great Depression, President Franklin Roosevelt's New Deal provided work for thousands through the WPA's building of roads, bridges, buildings, parks, and stadiums. Thankfully, many of these WPA-built structures here in Toledo have retained their grand facades while undergoing facelifts or creative reuse. Today, Toledoans are proud to point them out and brag about how their family members helped build them.

LAUGH AND CRY
WITH THE TOLEDO REPERTOIRE THEATRE

When you're craving a night out of local live theater, the Toledo Repertoire Theatre is the venue for you. Founded in 1933 to educate, entertain, and serve Toledo and the surrounding region through live theatre, the Rep is Toledo's first community theatre. The local troupe moved into its current location on 10th Street, originally a church, in 1934. Today, Toledo's enduring community theatre offers a wide variety of programming, including plays, musicals, staged readings, Young Rep productions (ages 7-19), classes, workshops, and the holiday favorite, *A Christmas Carol*.

Tickets are usually $35 and below—groups of 10 or more can get special discounts. The box office is open Monday through Friday, from 10 am to 2 pm and one hour before each performance.

16 10th St., (419) 243-9277, toledorep.org

CATCH A PLAY OR CONCERT
AT THE STRANAHAN THEATER AND GREAT HALL

The Stranahan Theater and Great Hall, commonly called the Stranahan, is a 2,424-seat state-of-the-art, multipurpose performing arts venue featuring entertainment at its best with Broadway, ballet, opera, lectures, symphony, and top-name performers gracing the stage. Built in 1969 and named after the family that brought Champion Spark Plug Company to Toledo, the Stranahan hosts a variety of great entertainment. Recent performances include Broadway productions of *Wicked* and *Harry Potter and the Sorcerer's Stone*, and outstanding concerts featuring Vince Gill, Steely Dan, and Los Lobos.

So, what's up with "Great Hall" in our description? The theater's foyer is 3,000 square feet, and the adjacent Great Hall features 10,000 square feet of meeting space for conferences, banquets, and receptions.

4645 Heatherdowns Blvd., (419) 381-8851, stranahantheater.com

CHECK OUT ART
IN PUBLIC PLACES

Toledo enjoys an impressive collection of public art, with large-scale sculptures, murals, and functional structures by noted artists from across the country. Many of these pieces were acquired through the pioneering 1977 ordinance that set aside 1% of the city's Capital Improvement Budget for the purchase, conservation, and public education of art.

The Arts Commission administers this innovative program through its Art in Public Places Program, which acquires, conserves, and restores the collection. The Arts Commission's administration also includes the education of the community related to the understanding and enjoyment of public art. Go online to pick up a self-guided tour of more than 100 public art pieces on display in Toledo.

Art in Public Places, (419) 254-ARTS (2787)
theartscommission.org/publicart

CHASE THE BLUES AWAY
AT GRIFFIN HINES FARMS

If you're looking to enjoy some cold beer, outstanding barbecue, and live blues music in a historic outdoor venue, head for Hines Farm out by the Gene Kranz Airport in Swanton. Hines Farm has been bringing good people, great music, and delicious food together for more than 60 years! Some of the finest blues musicians, such as B. B. King, Freddy King, John Lee Hooker, Bobby "Blue" Bland, Little Esther Phillips, Jimmy Ricks, the Griswold Brothers, and many more have played inside these walls, making "The Farm" one of the most legendary blues clubs around!

3950 Berkey Southern Rd., Swanton, (419) 320-0216

CELEBRATE OUTDOOR GIGS
AT PROMENADE PARK

Famous for "Party in the Park" on Friday nights, this grassy waterside green provides benches, paths, a seating hill, and a pavilion featuring community events and concerts. Recently rejuvenated, Promenade Park sits next to the ProMedica headquarters, a refurbished late 19th-century steam-driven powerhouse along Toledo's downtown riverfront. The park hosts a popular outdoor summer concert series with class acts such as Chaka Khan, Diana Ross, En Vogue, and Kid N' Play. Local beer and food trucks provide superb food and libations to make the Promenade Park concert experience a night to remember. Tickets are available through the Huntington Center box office or Ticketmaster.

400 Water St., (419) 245-3357, promenadeconcerts.com

ROCK THE HOUSE
AT THE HUNTINGTON CENTER

The Huntington Center is an 8,000-seat multipurpose arena in downtown Toledo. Completed in 2009 at a cost of $105 million, it's home to the Toledo Walleye hockey team and plays host to 36 regular-season home games each season.

The state-of-the-art facility has become a premier stop-off for national touring concerts and performances, including musicians from every genre, world-renowned family shows, and local, state, and regional sporting events. The Huntington Center has been named the top multipurpose arena in the Midwest by industry magazine *Venues Today*.

500 Jefferson Ave., (419) 255-3000, huntingtoncentertoledo.com

Photo courtesy of Destination Toledo

SPORTS AND RECREATION

HIT A HOME RUN
WITH THE TOLEDO MUD HENS

The Toledo Mud Hens are Toledo's professional Minor League Baseball team affiliated with the Detroit Tigers, based about 50 miles north of Toledo. They play their home games at Fifth Third Field. If you are looking for a great night out with the family, you'll love experiencing America's pastime with all the peanuts, popcorn, hot dogs, and more at what's been voted one of the best ballparks in America. Most weekend nights include a free fireworks display against the backdrop of the Toledo skyline.

Located adjacent to the ballpark on N St. Clair Street, you'll find Hensville, a new and exciting chapter in the transformation of Toledo's Warehouse District. Developed and managed by the Mud Hens, Hensville features three historic properties that offer entertainment for the entire family, ranging from concerts and live performances to private party spaces, rooftop decks, and more.

406 Washington St., (419) 725-4367, milb.com/toledo

WATCH 'EM TRADE PAINT
AT TOLEDO SPEEDWAY

Toledo Speedway is home to a half-mile oval asphalt racetrack that delivers high-octane entertainment on Friday nights from May through September. The track is operated by ARCA and run as the sister track to Flat Rock Speedway in Flat Rock, Michigan. The speedway hosts professional racers from the ARCA Menards and USAC Silver Crown Series and ARCA Sportsman, Street Stock, Figure 8, and Factory Stock Series for local racers throughout their season. This is a cheap night out with plenty of cold beer, hot dogs, and other concessions to go along with the high-speed racing. A no-alcohol family seating area is also available in the main grandstand.

5639 Benore Rd., (419) 725-4367, toledospeedway.com

GRAB A DRINK AND THROW A FEW ROCKS
AT THE BLACK SWAMP CURLING CLUB

The Black Swamp Curling Center opened its doors in 2017, becoming the new, permanent home for the Bowling Green Curling Club. With four sheets of dedicated curling ice, a viewing room, and a full bar called The 9th End, Black Swamp is the only dedicated curling center in northwest Ohio.

Guests and spectators are always welcome to visit and watch live curling games. Seasonal league games are played from October to April. Black Swamp also hosts several bonspiels and competitions throughout the year, learn to curl classes, corporate team building events, and a thriving junior curling program. They also sell Learn-to-Curl gift certificates!

19901 N Dixie Highway, Bowling Green, bgcurlingclub.com

GET HOOKED
ON T-TOWN HOCKEY
AT A WALLEYE GAME

The Toledo Walleye are members of the Central Division of the Western Conference of the ECHL. The Walleye were founded in 1991 as the Toledo Storm and play their home games at the Huntington Center.

Whether you're a die-hard hockey fan or just a sports enthusiast looking to have a great time, nothing compares to being part of a boisterous, sold-out crowd cheering on their hometown Walleye at the Huntington Center. I guarantee after just one game, you'll know without a doubt how to answer the question, "Hey, T-Town! Are you ready?"

Huntington Center, (419) 725-9255, toledowalleye.com

ROLL A STRIKE
AT JUG'S BOWLING CENTER

Toledo and bowling go hand in hand. The Glass City has a rich bowling history that goes back more than 100 years. Raymond Jakubowski Sr., also known as "Mr. Jug's," bought 13 acres of land on Jackman Road in the 1950s, and after a little influence from Bob Beach, a bowling writer for the Blade at the time, he jumped into the bowling business. Jug's Bowling Center opened in August of 1956. After more than 60 years of operation, what started as a 16-lane bowling center expanded to 24 lanes and features a first-class grill and pro shop. Jug's hosts bowling leagues and tournaments for all ages and is a great place for throwing birthday parties and other celebrations.

511 Jackman Rd., (419) 472-8260, jugsbowling.com

ROOT FOR THE ROCKETS
AT THE GLASS BOWL

The Toledo Rockets football team is a Division I FBS college football program representing the University of Toledo. The Rockets compete in the Mid-American Conference. Toledo began playing football in 1917, and their football program is an integral part of our region's strong sports culture.

The Glass Bowl, a WPA-built jewel refurbished a few years ago, is located on the school's Bancroft campus, just south of the banks of the Ottawa River. If you are a fan of college football, you won't want to miss the excitement, tradition, and high-quality competition that is Rocket football!

1745 Stadium Dr., (419) 472-8260, utrockets.com

PLAY THE FIRST PUBLIC GOLF COURSE WEST OF NEW YORK
AT OTTAWA PARK

No public course in the area can rival the beauty and classic style of Ottawa Park, the first public golf course west of New York. In 1922, it hosted the first US Amateur Public Links Championship. The municipal course, while short, still tests today's golfers with its tree-lined fairways and well-crafted greens. As you walk the course, you can feel its history.

2315 Walden Pond Rd., (419) 472-2059, toledocitygolf.com

TIP

Not a stick and ball kind of person? Don't let that stop you from enjoying Ottawa Park. They have the ONLY disc golf course in Toledo, one of only five disc golf courses in northwest Ohio and southeast Michigan. The course was constructed by the city in 1995, using a design provided by the Toledo Area Disc Golf Association (TADGA).

It's free to play, no tee times, and open year-round. TADGA salts and shovels the tees in the winter.

TIP

Northwest Ohio is home to more than 50 challenging golf courses, including the following great public and private links:

Inverness Club
Regularly rated among the top 100 courses in the world, designed by Donald Ross.
4601 Dorr St., invernessclub.com

Sylvania Country Club
Where Nicklaus first met Palmer at the 1954 Ohio Amateur Championship, designed by Willie Park Jr.
5201 Corey Rd., Sylvania, sylvaniacc.org

Stone Ridge Golf Club
Featuring rolling hills with stunning vistas, designed by Arthur Hills.
1553 Muirfield Dr., Bowling Green, stoneridgegolfclub.org

The Legacy Golf Club
Includes five bodies of water and narrow fairways, designed by Arthur Hills.
7677 New US 223, Ottawa Lake, MI, playlegacy.com

Maumee Bay State Park Golf Course
A Scottish-links style layout designed by Arthur Hills.
1750 Park Rd. 2, Oregon
maumeebaylodge.com/recreation/golf

Highland Meadows Golf Club
Home of the LPGA Marathon Classic since 1989, designed by Sandy Alves.
7455 Erie St., Sylvania, hmgolfclub.org

Toledo Country Club
The oldest Toledo-area private club, designed by Willie Park Jr.
3949 River Rd., toledocountryclub.com

INDULGE IN SOME COLLEGE HOOPS
AT SAVAGE ARENA

If you're looking for something to do inside during the cold Northwest Ohio winter, you'll warm up quickly, cheering on the University of Toledo Rockets men's basketball team as they play opponents from the Mid American Conference at Savage Arena. Besides taking on rivals from the MAC, the Rockets also face a formidable lineup of college basketball powerhouses from across the country each season, including Notre Dame, Bradley, and Howard, to name just a few. You'll enjoy some high-level, excellent gameplay at a very reasonable price; gameday tickets run from $11 to $23.50.

The UT Rockets have played in four NCAA March Madness tournaments and earned nine NIT appearances. John F. Savage Arena, named after a local financial executive who led the campaign to raise funds for the university's Glass Bowl Renovation Project, is a multi-purpose arena located on the UT campus. It features a "bowl-style" seating configuration that brings fans close to the action. The hall opened in 1976 and received a $30 million renovation in 2008. It seats about 7,300 for basketball and up to 8,300 for concerts.

2025 North Douglas Rd., (419) 472-8260, utrockets.com

Photo courtesy of Destination Toledo

GET A KICK OUT OF LIFE
AT PACESETTER PARK'S SOCCER FIELDS

If you're a soccer family, you'll be amazed at Sylvania Pacesetter Park's 138-acre multiuse sports complex. This facility hosts many youth soccer teams and adult leagues, as well as several local and regional tournaments each year. The entire facility is maintained with the highest care, offering daily practice fields, competition game fields, and eight fully lighted baseball and softball diamonds.

This beautiful park includes full concession stands and restroom facilities along with an 18,000-square-foot playground, a 30,000-square-foot Skate Plaza, and a 1.5-mile walking/jogging path.

8801 Sylvania-Metamora Rd., Sylvania, (419) 885-1982
playsylvania.com

FISH THE WALLEYE RUN
ON THE MAUMEE RIVER

As winter gives up her grip on northwest Ohio, anglers flock from across the country to the Maumee River to catch their share during the legendary Maumee River Walleye Run. Just when the water temperature, flow rate, and length of the day tell them it's time to spawn, hundreds of thousands of walleye head up the Maumee to return to where life began. The combination of the rising spring runoff waters and a river bottom of small rocks and gravel make for excellent walleye spawning grounds. The Maumee boasts the largest population of migrating walleye east of the Mississippi River.

Most of the good fishing action occurs from Orleans Park in Perrysburg to Side Cut Metropark from mid-March through April. You'll find plenty of vendors hawking their unique lures and jigs along River Road during the spring run.

Between Maumee and Waterville, maumeeriverwalleyerun.com

MAKE A BET
AT THE HOLLYWOOD CASINO

Toledo's rich history of high rollers goes back to the beginning of the twentieth century. By the 1940s, we were home to Club Devon, the largest and most elaborate gambling facility in the United States—decades before gambling was legal!

Today, if you're looking to try your luck at slots and table games or having a great meal and live music, Hollywood Casino is the place to go in Toledo. In addition to 2,000 slot machines, 60 table games, and a 20-table live poker room, this 125,000-square-foot casino boasts five restaurants, including Final Cut Steak & Seafood, Epic Buffet, and the Jim Beam American Steakhouse.

1968 Miami St., (419) 661-5200, hollywoodcasinotoledo.com

CATCH YOUR LIMIT OF PERCH ON LAKE ERIE
WITH THE WEST SISTER CHARTER FLEET

Lake Erie is known for its superior walleye fishing, and the West Sister Charter Fleet anchored at Anchor Point Marina offers the finest in walleye charters Lake Erie has to offer. Take your pick of 15 elite fishermen who have a lifetime of experience and absolutely love what they do! Most of these captains have been fishing in Lake Erie well over 30 years now. These well-seasoned pros fish the Western Lake Erie Basin every day (April to November) for its abundant selection of the desirable and massive walleye and our world-famous Lake Erie perch.

10955 Corduroy Rd., Curtice, wscba.com

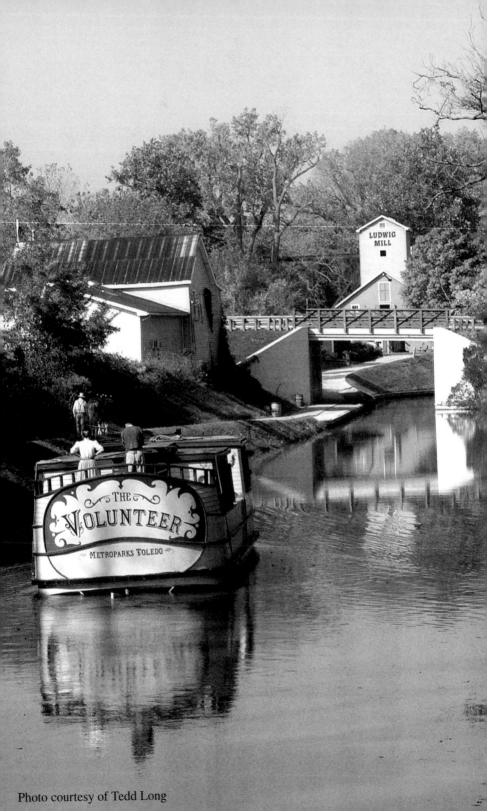

Photo courtesy of Tedd Long

CULTURE AND HISTORY

CELEBRATE THE GREAT LAKES
AT THE NATIONAL MUSEUM OF THE GREAT LAKES

Toledo may be well-known for its incredible art museum, but we are also home to one of the finest nautical museums in North America. Located on the banks of the Maumee River just across from downtown Toledo, the National Museum of the Great Lakes tells the incredible story of our Great Lakes through more than 300 genuine artifacts, powerful audiovisual displays, and 40 hands-on interactive exhibits, including a submarine dive on the wreck of the *Edmund Fitzgerald*. The NMGL galleries detail the role of the great lakes in Native American culture, white settlement, military history, the rise of American agriculture and industry, and the evolution of maritime technology.

Plan on setting aside several hours for your visit to the museum. If you are visiting during May through October, add some additional time so you can also tour a gigantic Great Lakes freighter, the S.S. *Col. James Schoonmaker*, and *The Ohio*, a retired Great Lakes tugboat.

1701 Front St., (419) 214-5000, nmgl.org

GET WILD
AT THE TOLEDO ZOO

Everyone loves to visit the Toledo Zoo & Aquarium to see their favorite animals and enjoy the innovative exhibits. Offering a wonderful collection of WPA-era historic buildings with more than 5,300 animals representing more than 760 species, our nationally ranked zoo includes one-of-a-kind areas such as the African savanna, featuring the Hippoquarium; the Kingdom of the Apes and Primate Forest; and the Arctic Encounter—all in a beautiful open-air setting.

With nearly 1 million visitors each year, the Toledo Zoo is northwest Ohio's most-visited attraction. It's open year-round, excluding Thanksgiving, Christmas, and New Year's Day. Summer hours (May through Labor Day) are from 10 am to 5 pm. The zoo is open from 10 am to 4 pm the rest of the year, except for the holidays when it is open until 8 pm for the Lights Before Christmas, Toledo's favorite holiday tradition featuring more than a million sparkling lights, animated displays, the exhilarating Ice Slide, visits with Santa, and more!

2 Hippo Way, (419) 385-5721, toledozoo.org

ADMIRE WORLD-CLASS FINE ART
AT THE TOLEDO MUSEUM OF ART

Your visit to the Glass City would not be complete without a tour of the Toledo Museum of Art (TMA), one of America's finest museums exhibiting 30,000 masterworks spanning European and American art. Since its founding by glassmaker Edward Drummond Libbey and his wife Florence Scott Libbey in 1901, TMA has earned an international reputation for the excellence of its collection, its ground-breaking and wide-ranging education programs, and its beautiful and architecturally significant campus.

Thanks to the generosity of its founders, as well as the continued support of its members, TMA remains a privately endowed, nonprofit institution offering free access to its collection. Your visit to the museum's 35 galleries will showcase outstanding art from all over the world. You'll experience paintings and sculptures by Bearden, Cézanne, Calder, Degas, van Gogh, El Greco, Matisse, Monet, Picasso, Rembrandt, and Rubens, as well as masterworks from antiquity and Asia. Private docent-led tours are available by appointment.

2445 Monroe St., (419) 255-8000, toledomuseum.org

TIP

When you visit TMA, make sure you leave time in your schedule to go to the postmodern Glass Pavilion. Opened in 2006, the 74,000-square-foot addition is home to TMA's world-renowned glass collection. The Glass Pavilion features more than 5,000 works of art from ancient to contemporary times. Glassblowing demonstrations are offered daily.

TAKE A WALK
IN VICTORIAN AND EDWARDIAN
SPLENDOR IN THE OLD WEST END

Enjoy a GPS-guided tour of the rich and glorious history and architecture of Toledo's Old West End, featuring 25 city blocks of one of the largest collections of late Victorian and Edwardian homes left standing in the United States. This tour offers an insider's look at prominent figures such as Edward Drummond Libbey, who created a glass dynasty that conferred on our town its charming moniker, the Glass City.

Frank Lloyd Wright studied this area in planning his Oak Park Project in Illinois. The Old West End offers pristine examples of Colonial, Georgian, Italian Renaissance, Queen Anne, Dutch Colonial, French Second Empire, and Arts and Crafts homes. This walking tour offers three unique routes to explore the Old West End.

Old West End Stroll, oldwestendtours.com

HONOR TOLEDO'S FINEST
AT THE TOLEDO POLICE MUSEUM

The odd shape of the brick building in Ottawa Park offers the first clue that the Toledo Police Museum is one of the quirkiest and most fascinating stops for anyone interested in Toledo history. This gallery offers interactive exhibits and a cool timeline display highlighting the Toledo Police Department's history, going back to 1837. Several rotating exhibits tell the stories of special units and individual officers who served the Toledo community. The artifacts on display include a 1948 police wagon, counterfeit money, confiscated weapons (including the gun used by the notorious Licavoli Gang to kill Toledo bootlegger Jack Kennedy during the Unholy Toledo era), a replica of Old Sparky (Ohio's electric chair), photographs, uniforms, a call box, badges, and handwritten police records.

The Toledo Police Museum is situated in Ottawa Park, directly next door to a playground and the Liz Pierson Picnic Shelter. You should set aside a few hours to enjoy this interesting venue. Don't miss the Police Museum's annual Cops and Rodders Car Show each June if you are into classic cars—it's one of the area's best car shows.

2201 Kenwood Blvd., (419) 720-2485, toledopolicemuseum.com

FUEL YOUR FIRE FOR HISTORY
AT THE TOLEDO FIREFIGHTERS MUSEUM

The Toledo Firefighters Museum is a great place to learn about a part of Toledo we all admire and respect, but most hope never to have to experience. Founded in 1976 and housed in the "Old Number 18 Fire House" built in 1920, this museum preserves the Toledo Fire Division's history and educates the public about fire prevention and safety. The Firefighters Museum's exhibits, along with the help of retired firefighter docents, tell the stories of Toledo's fire safety efforts from the 1800s to the present day. If your kids are into fire trucks, they'll get to see Toledo's first pumper engine, which was pulled by hand in 1837, as well as a later horse-drawn model. A simulated dispatch center demonstrates the evolution of operations inside the station, recalling days when telegraphs trumped telephones. You'll also experience an interactive fire training room on the second floor.

Covering more than 150 years of Toledo firefighting history, the Fire Museum's exhibits include antique toys, vintage uniforms, a watchman's desk, a command officer's room, and firefighters' sleeping quarters. This place is a terrific experience for kids and adults.

918 W Sylvania Ave., (419) 478-3473, toledofirefightersmuseum.org

POWER
YOUR KIDS' DREAMS
AT IMAGINATION STATION

Imagination Station is a nonprofit, hands-on science museum located on the Maumee riverfront in downtown Toledo. The science center is dedicated to making science, technology, engineering, and mathematics fun and accessible for children of all ages. There are hundreds of interactive, hands-on exhibits, activities, and demonstrations that are fun and educational for the entire family. Whether you only have an hour or you have all day, there is plenty to see and do here.

My favorite activity at Imagination Station is the high wire cycle, but the new KeyBank Discovery Theater featuring large-format movies should be on your list of things to do here too.

1 Discovery Way, (419) 244-2674, imaginationstationtoledo.org

SEE MORE THAN 1,000 BUTTERFLIES
AT THE BUTTERFLY HOUSE

With more than 1,000 butterflies from as far away as South America and Asia, the Butterfly House's controlled environment lets you view more than 100 species of the colorful insects that most of us only see in books or on television. Guests also learn about the butterfly's life cycle and how to attract them to your garden.

Whether you're hanging out on one of the many benches sprinkled throughout the enclosure or enjoying a relaxing stroll in the gardens, the butterflies are everywhere! Throughout their May through September season, the Butterfly House sponsors several events, including a monarch egg hunt and a popular monarch release program. Keep in mind that they offer group reservations for birthday parties, school field trips, senior citizen gatherings, and weddings. No doubt about it, the Butterfly House is a top 10 choice for entertaining kids in Toledo.

11455 Obee Rd., Whitehouse, (419) 877-2733
wheelerfarms.com/butterfly-house

TOUR AMERICA'S LARGEST WOODEN-WALLED FORTIFICATION
AT FORT MEIGS

The first thing most people notice after walking through the massive wooden gates of Fort Meigs is the sheer size of the largest wooden-walled reconstructed fortification in North America. It's hard to imagine how challenging it was to build this garrison in the harsh winter setting of February 1813.

Three main features make up this excellent local history destination. First is the Visitor Center housing an education center, restrooms, and vending machines. The main feature of the Visitor Center is the Museum Store, offering souvenirs, unique gifts, and one of the area's best local history bookstores. Second is the museum exhibit called "Legacy of Freedom: Fort Meigs in the War of 1812," which helps relate the fascinating story of Fort Meigs with hundreds of original artifacts on display, many of which were discovered as archaeologists investigated the grounds before the fort's reconstruction. Finally, there's the fort itself. It is awe-inspiring and features six blockhouses, each offering a unique story about the fort and the soldiers who lived and died there.

29100 W River Rd., Perrysburg, (419) 874-4121, fortmeigs.org

• •

FOLLOW HISTORY'S PATH
AT THE BATTLE OF FALLEN TIMBERS BATTLEFIELD

Toledo offers several impressive historical sites to explore, but the most historically significant is the Fallen Timbers Battlefield. Located near what is now Maumee, this battleground is where General Anthony Wayne's Legion defeated an American Indian confederacy on August 20, 1794, ending British territorial claims and sealing the Northwest Territory's fate through the Treaty of Greenville in 1795. Some say this was the last battle of the American Revolution.

To truly wrap your arms around the Fallen Timbers narrative, you should plan to set aside the better part of a day to visit three sites in northwest Ohio: the historic Fallen Timbers Battlefield Metropark off North Jerome Road, the handsome Fallen Timbers State Memorial overlooking the Maumee River off of US 24, and Fort Miamis, a British fortification that played a crucial role in the Battle of Fallen Timbers and the 1813 siege of Fort Meigs. All three sites offer first-rate, do-it-yourself opportunities to explore the Fallen Timbers story with wayfinding signs, interpretive displays, and walking paths.

The Battle of Fallen Timbers trilogy should be on everyone's local history itinerary.

I-475 & US 24, Maumee, (419) 407-9700, nps.gov/fati

TIP

Visitors can have their National Parks Passport stamped at the Maumee Branch of the Toledo-Lucas County Public Library, located on River Road.

STEP BACK IN TIME
WITH HERITAGE SYLVANIA

Another couple of excellent history venues to explore in the Toledo area are managed by Heritage Sylvania. This nonprofit history center offers the Sylvania Historical Village, the Lathrop House, and the Heritage Center Museum for unique visits back in time. The Historical Village includes original and replica historic structures to tell the story of Sylvania's early days as a farming village before it became a Toledo suburb. The Lathrop House provides a glimpse into the Underground Railroad as docents lead tours of this station, including its secret passage to a basement where runaway slaves hid while on their journey to freedom in Canada. The Heritage Center Museum offers rotating exhibits and the opportunity to explore early 20th-century life in the home and office of Dr. Uriah Cooke.

5717 Main St., Sylvania, (419) 517-5533, heritagesylvania.org

MAKE YOURSELF AT HOME
AT THE SPAFFORD HOUSE MUSEUM

Once inside this historic home, the oldest standing wood-frame house in Perrysburg, you'll quickly appreciate the attention to detail that went into the restoration of the Spafford House Museum. The early American Greek Revival house was originally built in 1823 by Aurora Spafford, son of Amos Spafford, founder of Perrysburg. While the house was moved a few feet from its original foundation during restoration, it appears unaltered on its lot in the Spafford Land Grant just a few hundred feet west of Fort Meigs and above the now-vanished river town of Orleans of the North.

Today, Spafford House guests enjoy beautifully restored rooms arranged with original furnishings, clothing, hand-crafted fixtures, and period artifacts dating back to the 1790s. The museum includes a room dedicated to first responders and members of the armed services from the Perrysburg area and space devoted to American Indian artifacts. The second floor features a one-room schoolhouse display.

The Spafford House Museum is a fun and thought-provoking stop to include on your Perrysburg area tour and can fit easily into a day trip to Fort Meigs.

27340 W River Rd., Perrysburg, (419) 931-0910
perrysburgmuseum.com

TOUR
THE ART LOOP

Toledo's creative spirit is on display throughout the city, and one significant way we nurture our arts culture is through the city's Arts Commission. Our Arts Commission is Ohio's oldest, serving the artists and creatives of Greater Toledo since 1959.

Our innovative and influential Arts Commission curates a monthly Art Loop. This signature experience explores the downtown creative community through self-guided tours and events that help engage attendees in arts and cultural experiences. The best way to attend the Art Loop is to visit the Arts Commission's website, check out their calendar for details, and then plan your exploration.

1838 Parkwood Ave., Suite 120, (419) 254-2787, theartscommission.org

MEET SOME GANGSTERS
ON THE UNHOLY TOLEDO TOUR

If you've ever wondered about Toledo's unholiest gangsters, the Glass City's infamous "Tenderloin" district, or the town's most notorious gambling halls—you'll want to take the Unholy Toledo Tour. This gangster tour uses a phone app called VoiceMap and your GPS-enabled phone as your guide, so you and your guests can enjoy the expedition from the comfort of your own vehicle. This narrated tour uses music and sound effects to create a moving podcast that provides a unique trip back to Toledo as it was during the "unholy" years. You'll explore historically accurate accounts of the Licavoli Gang, the Detroit mob that invaded Toledo during Prohibition. You'll also follow the stories of Jack Kennedy, Jimmy Hayes, and a cast of other characters from Toledo's bawdy past as you cruise the streets in search of the old hoodlum haunts, brothels, gambling dens, and sites of gangland shootouts.

This "DIY" tour is about 20 miles in length, consists of 22 stops, and takes about two hours to complete.

unholytoledotour.com

ENJOY LIFE AT A SLOW AND EASY PACE
AT SAUDER VILLAGE

Erie J. Sauder founded the Sauder Woodworking Company in 1934, and, today, it's known as a global leader in ready-to-assemble furniture. Although known as a forward-thinking innovator, Sauder enjoyed a keen appreciation for the past. In the 1970s, after making a success of his business and looking forward to retirement, Sauder invested in the local area to ensure that future generations could appreciate the local pioneers' hard work and sacrifice to settle northwest Ohio. At his instruction, dozens of structures, built by hand a century earlier, were moved from locations throughout the area to create Sauder Village in Archbold.

As Ohio's largest living history destination, Sauder Village now features costumed interpreters, hands-on demonstrations, and curated exhibits. Take a walk through the early 1800s to 1920s as you tour historic homes, working farms, a 1920s Main Street, and the various shops that reflect the village's genial character. In the village, you can interact with interpreters and craftspeople who stand ready to tell their stories, share an old-world craft, or ask for your help shelling beans or making butter.

22611 OH Route 2, Archbold, (800) 590-9755, saudervillage.org

TIP

If you make a day of your trip to Sauder Village, don't miss the Barn Restaurant's homestyle meals and homemade baked goods at the Doughbox Bakery, or pack a picnic and enjoy it on the Village Green or Picnic Shelter. If you're staying over, you'll find readily available first-class camping and overnight accommodations as well.

CELEBRATE EAST TOLEDO'S HUNGARIAN CULTURE
AT THE BIRMINGHAM FESTIVAL

One of Toledo's oldest and most popular ethnic festivals, the Birmingham Ethnic Festival—"A Weekend in the Old Country" has been held the third weekend in August for the past 45 years to celebrate the strength and diversity of the East Toledo community and to support the continuing fight for the preservation and recognition of the historic neighborhood.

This weekend festival features food, music, dance, and shopping to bring back memories of Toledo's Birmingham neighborhood. My favorite foods at this festival are the stuffed cabbage, homemade kolbász sandwiches, and szalonna sutes, affectionately dubbed Hunky Turkey and made from roasted bacon. If you want a complete meal, try the chicken paprikás dinners sold on Saturday (starting at 4:30 pm) and Sunday at Calvin United, and at St. Stephen's Hall from 12 pm–3 pm (or until they run out).

Consaul St., facebook.com/BirminghamEthnicFestival/

LAP UP FOOD, DRINK, AND DANCE
AT THE GERMAN AMERICAN FESTIVAL

Toledoans love their ethnic festivals, and the Germans like to brag that theirs, held in late August each year, is the biggest and oldest in the area. Frankly, I couldn't care less which festival is the biggest or oldest; the fact is this festival is Toledo's epicenter for savoring delicious German food, imported beer, and experiencing authentic German music, folk dancing, and entertainment. Want to go beyond food and beer? Try your hand in some of the traditional contests and feats such as the Steinstossen, a centuries-old Swiss stone-throwing tournament. Or enjoy the folk dancing and the magical moment at the top of each hour when dancers emerge to perform a comedy routine while they strike the chimes on the giant glockenspiel. There are also lots of fun interactive activities and rides for the kids.

Toledo's German American Festival has been promoting the German and Swiss cultures and providing a fabulous time for festival-goers of all ages for more than half a century. Don't miss it. Prost!

3624 Seaman Rd., Oregon, (419) 691-4116
germanamericanfestival.net

HOLLER "OPA"
AT THE GREEK AMERICAN FESTIVAL

Not to be outdone by the other ethnic festivals in Toledo, the Greek American Festival features authentic Greek food, pastries, and dancing while offering Greek boutiques, education booths, and tours of the beautiful Byzantine Cathedral.

The food is the star at this festival, and Toledo's Greek culinary experts are happy to share their secrets with free Greek language culture presentations and their popular Greek cooking demonstrations. Hosted by the Holy Trinity Greek Orthodox Cathedral, the festival is held in early September each year.

740 N Superior St., (419) 243-9189, toledogreekfest.com

REVEL IN FAMILY FUN
AT THE TOLEDO AFRICAN AMERICAN PARADE AND FESTIVAL

When this festival started in 2005 at the corner of Detroit and Indiana, just a few hundred people showed up. Today, this much-anticipated celebration has blossomed into a major summer event hosting thousands. Held the third weekend in July, the Toledo African American Parade and Festival celebrates African American life, history, and heritage, beginning with a prayer breakfast and gospel concert on Friday morning. The parade and festival kick-off along Dorr Street on Saturday and more festivities follow on Sunday.

This festival has it all: a parade, live music, plenty of delicious food and drink, and lots of family-fun activities.

SeaGate Convention Center, (419) 255-8876, toledourban.net

SEE HOW TOLEDO'S GLASS PIONEERS LIVED
AT THE LIBBEY HOUSE

Edward Drummond Libbey married Toledo's Florence Scott in 1890, after moving his family's glass business from the Boston area to Toledo two years earlier. The up-and-coming couple soon commissioned local architect David L. Stine to plan their new home, and construction was completed in 1895. Today, this beautiful shingle and Colonial Revival–style home anchors Toledo's historic Old West End neighborhood's southern border with the Toledo Museum of Art campus.

The nearly 10,000-square-foot house features three floors, a cherry wood grand staircase, a mahogany parlor, and a paneled dining room accented by 10 hand-carved lion heads. Repeated throughout the house are dentil, egg and dart, and bead and reel moldings. And you can't miss the columns. There are Doric, Ionic, and Corinthian order columns inside and outside of the home. The beautiful solarium overlooks the Toledo Museum of Art—gifted to our community by the Libbeys.

The Libbey house serves as a one-of-a-kind venue for the Libbey House Foundation. This nonprofit group offers tours, events, and receptions to raise revenue to restore and preserve the National Historic Landmark. Tours are available by appointment.

2008 Scottwood Ave., (419) 252-0722, libbeyhouse.org

EXPERIENCE THE SHEER BEAUTY
OF OUR LADY, QUEEN OF THE MOST HOLY ROSARY CATHEDRAL

Inside and out, this is the most spectacular building in Toledo! It is one of only a few Plateresque (architectural style of 16-century Spain) cathedrals in the world, giving the nod to Toledo's sister city in Spain. Outside, this impressive cathedral's facade is a study of artistic detail with its statuary, delicate stone traceries, shields, arches, spires, and magnificent twin towers bearing their namesakes Peter and Paul, respectively. The oversized front doors are paneled European cypress, as are all the exterior doors, and decorated with stained glass and bronze rosettes. Above the porch is the enormous rose window's stonework, and above that, the diocesan coat of arms and the surmounting cross. The cathedral bells housed in both towers were cast at Croyden in England and are a poignant presence in Toledo's Old West End.

Inside, layers of paintings and frescoes of saints and angels reach the ceiling with a magnificent stained glass rose window and mosaic altars. From the floor to the ridge of the roof measures over 90 feet! The inside features a cream-colored Florido marble altar, wall and ceiling frescoes, stained glass windows, and a carved Black Forest white oak pulpit. I'm afraid my descriptions can't do the interior any justice. You really must experience the inside of this sanctuary!

2535 Collingwood Blvd., (419) 244-9575, rosarycathedral.org

EXPLORE TOLEDO'S BEAUTY AND ITS PAST
AT WOODLAWN CEMETERY & ARBORETUM

Toledo's Woodlawn Cemetery was founded in 1876 based on the principles of the rural cemetery movement. It features a charming lake, winding drives, gently rolling hills, impressive trees, and inspiring monuments. While some say Woodlawn no longer represents a true example of the rural cemetery movement because Toledo's swiftly growing boundaries absorbed the quiet retreat in the early 20th century, I believe it still exemplifies all the best points of this beautiful style.

If you've never ventured past the imposing iron gates of Woodlawn, you're missing out on one of Toledo's most inspiring places to visit. I highly recommend a walk through Woodlawn— any time of the year. As you stroll along the winding paths, you'll recognize notable names from Toledo's past such as Flower, Gunckel, Libbey, Reynolds, Secor, Spitzer, and Tiedtke, to name just a few. As a bonus to the elegant landscaping and architectural features that define its rural cemetery roots, Woodlawn is also a very popular birding area and home to more than 300 species of trees, making it one of the finest arboretums in northwest Ohio.

1502 W Central Ave., (419) 472-2186, historic-woodlawn.com

TIP

Woodlawn offers a free interactive smartphone tour at www.woodlawntour.com.

HIT THE BOOKS
AT MAIN LIBRARY

Designed by the architectural firm Hahn & Hayes, the Art Deco Main Library, featuring stunning Vitrolite murals in its main lobby, opened in 1940. Its $2 million cost was financed mainly by the WPA. This building replaced the city's original 1890 main library, located at Madison Avenue and Ontario Street, and hosts several departments, including Computers & Media, Children's Library, Fact & Fiction, Local History & Genealogy, and the Teen Department & Studio Lab. The Children's Library includes a Creativity Lab, Computer Center, Family School Readiness Room, and a Picture Book Room.

I know what you're thinking—why is a library on this list? Let me tell you, the Children's Library is the perfect place to bring young ones if you want to create lifelong learners, develop their brains, and spark their love of adventure and curiosity! Besides all that, it's loads of fun, and the staff is first-rate!

325 N Michigan Ave., (419) 259-5200, toledolibrary.org

TIP

Main Library also houses the award-winning Rogowski-Kaptur Labor History Room and the Blade Rare Book Room & Vault featuring rare and valuable items such as an 1800 letter from Thomas Jefferson and first editions of the original Nancy Drew series, written by a local newspaper columnist and author, Mildred Wirt Benson. These rooms are located in my favorite part of the library, the Local History and Genealogy Department.

SLEEP IN A TREE
AT THE METROPARKS CANNALEY TREEHOUSE VILLAGE

The Treehouse Village at Oak Openings Preserve provides Metroparks visitors memorable experiences that connect people with nature in ways you can't find anywhere else. With help from Nelson Treehouse and Supply, of the TV show *Treehouse Masters*, the Cannaley Treehouse Village features a six-person treehouse, a four-person treehouse, a couple of two-person treehouses, three tent/hammock platforms for camping in the trees, a common treehouse with seating for up to 49 people, a crow's nest, and a canopy walk linking the common treehouse to the crow's nest. All provide an unparalleled view of the nature surrounding them.

The four private treehouses and tent platforms are available to rent for an overnight stay, and the common treehouse is reservable for group gatherings.

Oak Openings Preserve, home of the Cannaley Treehouse Village, spanning nearly 5,000 acres, is the largest Metropark in the Toledo area. It is part of a corridor connecting five parks and three state nature preserves, protecting globally rare habitats of rare and endangered plants.

3520 Waterville Swanton Rd., Swanton, (419) 407-9700

metroparkstoledo.com

HIKE AND SLED
AT SIDE CUT

Side Cut is an idyllic picnic spot set in a deep ravine with rustic bridges and lagoons. Only the indifferent trickle of water through the old locks is left to recall when this was an "industrial suburb" of Maumee village. Here, canal boats were brought to the river level through six locks as a Maumee Side Cut. Of these locks, three remain, their huge gray stone blocks quarried from the Marblehead Peninsula of Lake Erie, and are solidly still in place. A brickyard, a flour mill, and a paper mill were also once located here.

Side Cut includes nearly seven miles of trails (not including the Wabash Cannonball Trail) and contains one of the best sledding hills in the flatlands of northwest Ohio. The park is also on every walleye angler's bucket list for the "spring run" of walleye each March and April.

1025 W River Rd., Maumee, (419) 360-9701
metroparkstoledo.com

WALK OR BIKE
YOUR WAY AROUND THE MIDDLEGROUNDS

Middlegrounds Metropark, the local park system's first urban park, is located in downtown Toledo. It includes a half-mile of river frontage that begins at the Anthony Wayne Bridge and extends southwest of Martin Luther King Plaza. The 28-acre green space offers a 1.5-mile meandering walk/bike path and tranquil views of the Maumee River.

Middlegrounds is a reclaimed riverfront property on a long span of filled-in land stretching down between the Maumee River and Swan Creek just south of downtown Toledo. Much of it was initially a shallow inlet from the river and contained a growth of wild rice before one of Toledo's first warehouses was built here. It acquired its name because it was a popular fishing grounds conveniently located on the "middle ground" between the river and Swan Creek. The transformation of the land into a park began with the removal of 8,000 tons of debris. Features were built with sustainability in mind. Unique elements include beautiful decking made of ipe wood, pronounced "ee-pay," a sustainable exotic wood from South America; a natural filter system that scrubs water runoff from the adjacent high-level bridge before it spills into the Maumee River. The 28-acre green space offers a peaceful respite from the hustle and bustle of downtown Toledo

111 Ottawa St., (419) 360-9714, metroparkstoledo.com

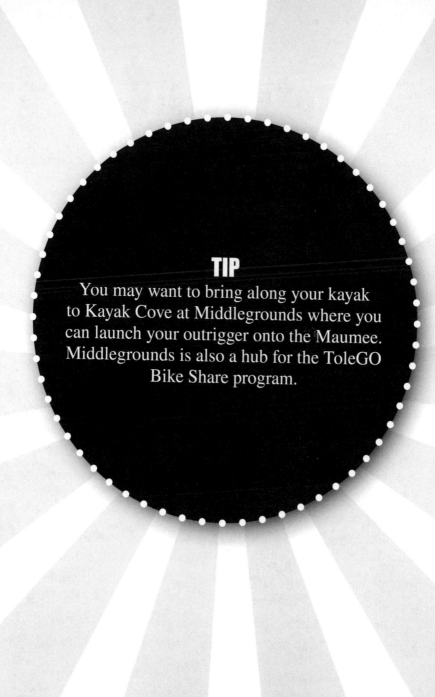

TIP

You may want to bring along your kayak to Kayak Cove at Middlegrounds where you can launch your outrigger onto the Maumee. Middlegrounds is also a hub for the ToleGO Bike Share program.

TAKE A WALK
ON THE WILD SIDE
AT WILDWOOD PRESERVE

If you are looking for a place to take a peaceful walk in the woods just outside the confines of the city, this 493-acre park, the former estate of R. A. Stranahan of Champion Spark Plugs, is the place to visit. Surrounded by beautiful natural habitat, Stranahan's stately Georgian Colonial home, now called the Manor House, serves as just one of several focal points in the area's most visited park. Wildwood's main attraction is the trails system that traverses several types of terrain—each trail offers a uniquely different experience. Features along the Wildwood trails include a covered bridge and the Ottawa River. The rolling wooded paths are perfect for hiking and jogging year-round and cross-country skiing during the winter months. There's also a beautiful prairie community at Wildwood that produces a spectacular display of wildflowers and grasses each summer.

Wildwood has a little something for everyone. There are a couple of fun playgrounds for the kids, bike paths, gazebos, benches for sitting, grills and picnic tables, and a marvelous window on wildlife, an indoor viewing area to watch an outdoor feeding station.

For me, Wildwood can sometimes get a little too crowded. No worries, we head west a few miles and visit Secor Metropark.

5100 W Central Ave., (419) 270-7500, metroparkstoledo.com

● ●

TIP

Need an outdoor workout? Try the FitPark equipped with workout stations designed for aerobic and balance exercise, core and muscle strengthening, and accessibility.

BUY A MASTERPIECE
AT THE CROSBY ARTS FESTIVAL

Toledo is all about the arts. To take home your own classic drawing, painting, or sculpture, visit the Crosby Festival of the Arts, our area's most popular fine arts show. Held on the beautiful grounds of the Toledo Botanical Gardens since 1965, this mid-summer festival is Ohio's oldest outdoor juried art festival and the premier fine arts festival in northwest Ohio. As the only show of its size and caliber in our region, juried artists are received enthusiastically by more than 10,000 visitors each year.

This three-day art show features beautiful artwork and great local food, drinks, live music, and enjoyable activities for children. I always suggest taking the free shuttle bus service to and from area shopping centers to avoid potential parking issues.

5403 Elmer Dr., (419) 720-8714, crosbyfest.com

INFUSE YOUR SOUL
WITH NATIVE AMERICAN VIBES AT A POWWOW

The Annual Woodland Indian Celebration at Buttonwood Park in Perrysburg is the premier Native American event in the region. This is an incredible chance to be a part of the beautiful Harvest Festival of the Eastern Woodland American Indians of the North East and Great Lakes. Every fall, we enjoy participating in Native American arts, crafts, dance, food, games, history, music, and more.

The Woodland Indian Celebration has been listed as one of the Top 20 Great Escapes: Weekends Worth Having in the State of Ohio by *Cincinnati Magazine* and has been named a State of Ohio Top Event by the Ohio Arts Council, the Ohio Humanities Council, and the *Toledo Blade*.

27174 Hull Prairie Rd., Perrysburg, (419) 353-1897
blackswampintertribalfoundation.org

FLOAT INTO THE PAST
AT THE CANAL EXPERIENCE

It's incredible how a one-hour boat ride can take you back over 140 years. That is the charm of the Canal Experience located near Providence Metropark in Grand Rapids. This site boasts one of the most significant concentrations of canal-era features in the country.

Your experience begins when you purchase a ticket for your canal adventure, and then board The Volunteer, a mule-drawn reproduction canal boat. Blink and it's suddenly 1876, and you are a passenger on the Miami-Erie Canal on your way to points south. Savvy historical interpreters in period costumes share stories of when the smoothest way to travel was aboard long, narrow wooden boats pulled by mules along man-made waterways. Your interpreters stay in character on the first half of the cruise as they manhandle your packet boat through Lock #44, one of the last functioning 19th-century limestone locks on the Miami and Erie Canal. After they make the turnaround up ahead, they break character and open up for questions and answers.

After your canal trip, a stop by the nearby Heritage Center and Isaac Ludwig Mill will round out your local history experience. The mill is a functioning water-powered saw and gristmill. Because milling was a part of my family's heritage for several generations, I enjoy talking with the costumed volunteers to learn more about how waterpower is used to saw wood, grind flour, and generate electricity.

13827 S River Rd., Grand Rapids, (419) 407-9700, metroparkstoledo.com

TIP

Plan to make a day out of your Canal Experience. Pack a picnic to enjoy in nearby Providence Metropark, and don't forget to bring your fishing poles to reel in some smallmouth bass at scenic Providence Dam (constructed across the Maumee River to maintain water levels in the canal). And make sure you leave yourself enough time to cross over the Maumee and visit Grand Rapids. This charming little canal town is known for its shops featuring antiques, collectibles, and unique gifts inside stunningly restored canal-era buildings, many of which are listed on the National Register of Historic Places.

CATCH A FLASH OF BLUE
AT KITTY TODD

While we're very fortunate to enjoy such an extraordinary chain of local Metroparks, our area is also home to the Nature Conservancy's Kitty Todd Preserve, a 1,400-acre centerpiece of the Oak Openings Region and a land management leader for our region. The Nature Conservancy is very committed to the Green Ribbon Initiative, an important regional partnership protecting our Oak Openings region's natural beauty and biological diversity.

Depending on the season, Kitty Todd has much to offer. As a nature photographer, I love the month of May when the preserve begins bursting with life and features plentiful blooms of wild blue lupine, the only plant upon which the federally endangered Karner blue butterfly feeds. Year-round activities include hiking, birding, wildlife-watching, nature photography, and native plant spotting.

10420 Old State Line Rd., Swanton, (419) 867-1521, nature.org

TAKE A SELFIE
AT "THE SPOT" IN OAK OPENINGS

The Spot is a tiny unmarked area in the middle of nowhere. Many people pass it up because it's not listed on any maps. It's about four acres of land in the middle of Oak Openings, where 1,200 red pine trees were planted more than 60 years ago to halt soil erosion. Oak Openings is the largest natural preserve in the Toledo area, known for its sand dunes and more rare plants and animals than anywhere else in Ohio. The Spot is located between Whitehouse and Swanton and is part of the Toledo Metroparks.

The Spot, which is not at all indicative of the rare natural surroundings of the Oak Openings, is nonetheless considered a cultural feature of the preserve because of visitors' affection for the neat rows of towering trees. It has become a magnet for photographers and a sensation on Instagram thanks to a unique configuration of pine trees and the stream of photographers from all over who have flocked to shoot it. The site has gained so much popularity that park officials bent their "stay on the trail" rules and posted signs leading to the photoshoot location. If you want specific directions, google "The Spot," and you'll find several sites directing you to the area in Oak Openings.

4139 Girdham Rd., Swanton, (419) 360-9179, instagram.com
#thenwospot

BUTTER SOME FUN
AT THE J. H. FENTRESS
ANTIQUE POPCORN MUSEUM

The J. H. Fentress Antique Popcorn Museum houses one of the largest and most diverse popcorn-related memorabilia collections in existence. It's a place to connect with the past and discover up close the ingenuity of our ancestors.

The Museum currently showcases more than 35 original Butter-Kist Popcorn machines and peanut roasters plus two Kist-Wich sandwich carts. Upwards of 70 striking signs and advertisements line the walls. Another unique exhibit sure to bring a smile to the faces of museumgoers of all ages are the delightful graphics on more than 300 old popcorn boxes, 200 popcorn tins, and 100 popcorn bags (both cellophane and burlap). There's even a private reading area where visitors who are doing machine restoration or simply intrigued by mechanics and design can peruse original manuals and detailed drawings of machines and machine parts.

7922 Hill Ave., Holland, (419) 308-4812
antiquepopcornmuseum.com

DISCOVER AN ALVAR
ON THE MIGHTY MAUMEE

There is a very rare habitat along the Maumee River between Maumee and Waterville called an alvar. It's made up of a limestone plain with thin or little soil that results in sparse grassland vegetation. Often flooded in the spring and affected by drought in midsummer, our Maumee River alvar supports a distinct group of prairie-like plants, lichen, and mosses. Most alvars occur either in northern Europe or around the Great Lakes in North America.

To visit, pull your car over on River Road just east of Jerome Road about a mile west of Side Cut Metropark. There are several trails leading out to the outcropping. Our grandkids and I like to visit in July and August when the river levels are just right, and there is plenty to explore.

Jerome Rd. and River Rd., between Maumee and Waterville

TAKE IN
A SPECTACULAR SUNSET
AT GRAND RAPIDS

Grand Rapids is a beautifully restored historic Victorian village located on the Maumee River's south bank, along the Historic Miami and Erie Canal.

This scenic river town is the perfect place to plan a "day-cation" to shop, play, dine, and stay. But don't forget the sunset along the Maumee River. Some of the best locations for photographs are along the dam on the Maumee's north bank off of US 24.

US 24, Grand Rapids, (419) 832-1106, visitgrandrapids.com

TIP

Looking to get a little closer to the water than shooting sunset photos from the shore, RiverLures Kayak Adventures in Grand Rapids provides full-service kayak trips on the Maumee. They use sit-on-tops, the safest boats on the water, and supply you with everything you need, including a shuttle ride back to their headquarters.

RiverLures Kayak Adventures
They also have a store in case you forget your sunscreen, snacks, or beverages.
24287 Front St., Grand Rapids, riverlureskayaking.com

Photo courtesy of Tedd Long

SHOPPING AND FASHION

SAVOR A CIGAR AND COCKTAIL
AT LA CASA DE LA HABANA

Offering one of the largest selections of premium cigars in the area with some of the best prices, La Casa De La Habana also has a fully stocked bar of top-shelf drinks. They stock an immense inventory of pipes and tobacco and cigar accessories, including lighters, cutters, ashtrays, and humidors. Owner Kyle Rahal is the cigar sommelier who oversees the wide-ranging collection of tobacco products and fine liquor at La Casa. He's always happy to help match you with your dream cigar.

Bring your friends and stay for awhile, relax, enjoy a cigar in the lounge, watch a soccer match on one of their big screen TV's, or get on the Internet with their free Wi-Fi. La Casa is all about having a memorable experience with good friends and great cigars!

4962 Monroe St., (419) 472-4427, lacasatoledo.com

SEARCH FOR VINTAGE CLOTHING
AT HOUSE OF DOW

The House of Dow is the area's premier shop for curated vintage clothing and accessories, available online and at their brick-and-mortar storefront in Uptown Toledo.

Allison Dow, House of Dow's founder, picked up her love of vintage from her mother. From an early age, she attended area estate sales with her mom and developed a keen eye for exciting pieces over time. Her unique products are unearthed from the depths of attics, abandoned warehouses, and estate sales, and are then given new life. If you get a chance to visit this store often, you'll notice that their stock is ever-changing—they add new merchandise online and to their Toledo storefront daily.

Are you having trouble finding that perfect vintage outfit? The House of Dow's in-house personal styling service caters to your shopping experience to help find that classic outfit or wardrobe that feels like you.

1501 Adams St., (419) 214-0944, houseofdow.com

PICK UP SOME HISTORY
AT ARCHITECTURAL ARTIFACTS

Are you looking for a place to find one-of-a-kind accoutrements for your home? Architectural Artifacts offers a fabulous array of salvaged antique and new architectural elements in wood, stone, marble, terra cotta, and iron. With an inventory that includes architectural salvage, doors, fireplaces, furniture, garden, hardware, industrial cool oddball items, lighting, plumbing, and windows, this place has all your restoration needs covered. You name it; they've got it. Just walking through the 30,000-square-foot store is an adventure.

Located in the historic Warehouse District and in business for more than 25 years—this place has tons of one-of-a-kind artifacts to include in your next restoration project.

Don't forget to say hello to Amy the cat. You'll find her lounging atop some columns or one of the antique tables.

20 S Ontario St., (419) 243-6915, coolstuffiscoolstuff.com

EXPAND YOUR HORIZONS
AT 20 NORTH GALLERY

Founded in 1993, 20 North Gallery is the oldest independent art gallery in Toledo. Located in a fully renovated historic building in the Warehouse District, this wonderful venue provides emerging and established local, regional, and international artists with a commercial venue to display and sell their work. The spacious gallery offers matchless ambiance with its 14-foot ceilings and original hardwood floors.

20 North Gallery represents both traditional and contemporary artists working in various media and offers residential and office consultations for art acquisition, placement, and installation. This gallery is a must-see for art lovers.

18 N St. Clair St., (419) 241-2400, 20northgallery.com

SUPPORT
LOCAL ARTISTS
AT HANDMADE TOLEDO

Toledo is known for its brilliant art scene, and this excellent art market is a marvelous outlet for the work of local and regional independent designers, makers, artisans, and DIYers. In addition to their Maker Shop, they host workshops, studios, and an enormously popular Maker's Mart twice a year, including their Maker's Mart Holiday Edition featuring more than 80 handmade vendors, local coffee and craft cocktails, beer, and a superb selection of delicacies from some of Toledo's best food truck vendors.

1717 Adams St., (419) 214-1717, handmadetoledo.com

RELIVE YOUR CHILDHOOD CANDY DREAMS
AT BOYD'S RETRO CANDY STORE

If you're searching for a true old-time candy store from your childhood, you absolutely must put Boyd's on your shopping list. Specializing in the '50s, '60s, and '70s but satisfying candy lovers of every generation, including candy going back to the 1800s, Boyd's will help you share a few childhood memories and make new ones with your kids. Where else can you savor that Curly Wurly or Cinnamon Dubble Bubble Gum Balls? Let Fizzies or Zotz tickle your tongue. Drink a refreshing Faygo, Crush, or Frostie Soda or one of the more unusual retro soda pops such as Nehi, Bubble Up, or Moxi.

Boyd's is also a cool place to treat your party or wedding guests to some of your childhood favorites. They'll work with you to put together a unique gift bag for your guests. As you can imagine, with more than 1,000 candy choices, I always walk into Boyd's intending to pick up just a few things, but I usually walk out with a bag chock-full of sweet memories.

954 Phillips Ave., (419) 720-7387, boydsretrocandy.com

GET FRESH
AT THE FARMERS MARKET

Our local Farmers Market of Toledo was started in 1832 when many of the area farmers needed a place to sell their produce and the community needed a centrally located place to shop. Over the years, the market has seen its ups and downs and sadly fell off most people's radars with the advent of super-sized grocery stores and large-capacity refrigeration.

Thankfully, today the Farmers Market is no longer Toledo's "best-kept secret." It offers an essential marketplace for local small family farms, agricultural producers, and artisans, whose continued existence depends on direct marketing opportunities. It has a bright look and is easily accessible to all, including the disabled.

My family enjoys visiting the market every Saturday. We often return for the special Thursday night offerings too. The food is always high quality, the fresh flowers are beautiful, and we always seem to find something different each week.

525 Market St., (419) 255-6754, toledofarmersmarket.com

TIP
The nearby Riverwalk along Swan Creek provides a nice place to relax while at the Farmers Market.

BRING HOME A T-SHIRT
OR TOLEDO SOUVENIR FROM JUPMODE

Jupmode is a custom decoration business and retail brand based in Toledo's Uptown neighborhood featuring cool, fun, vintage T-shirts, fleece, glassware, hats, and more. Their goal has always been to create and foster a sense of pride in Toledo by remembering our past and highlighting the new wave of excitement happening today.

As a local retail brand, Jupmode does its best to pay tribute to the hard work people have poured into Toledo and inspire others to make their mark. Their designers enjoy digging into Glass City history, finding vintage designs while also coming up with new designs representing the 419 (Toledo's area code). No matter your connection to Toledo, Jupmode will make you feel proud of this city and provide a terrific way to show off that pride.

2022 Adams St., (419) 318-2029, jupmode.com

TAKE HOME A GLASS CITY KEEPSAKE
FROM THE LIBBEY GLASS OUTLET STORE

Edward Libbey brought his father's glass legacy to Toledo in 1888 and made Toledo the Glass Capital of the World. The Libbey Glass Outlet offers visitors the chance to shop for beautiful glassware, serveware, stemware, dinnerware, barware, home décor items, and gift items from the top glassware company in the Americas and one of the largest tableware suppliers in the world.

The retail shop is located in the Warehouse District next to the Farmers Market and is open seven days a week.

205 Erie St., (419) 254-5000, retail.libbey.com

TIP

If you like to shop till you drop, the Glass City has you covered from shops that are independently owned and run to luxury boutiques. Bring along your wallet for a trip to one of Toledo's three large commercial centers, each offering its own unique shopping experience:

Franklin Park Mall
Macy's, Dillard's, JCPenney, and Dick's Sporting Goods anchor this mall.
5001 Monroe St.
(419) 473-3317, shoppingfranklinparkmall.com

The Town Center at Levis Commons
Open-air mall featuring more than 50 retailers and 15 restaurants.
3201 Levis Commons Blvd., Perrysburg
(419) 931-8888, shopleviscommons.com

The Shops at Fallen Timbers
An outdoor lifestyle center anchored by JCPenney, Dillard's, and Barnes & Noble.
3100 Main St., Maumee
(419) 740-7080, theshopsatfallentimbers.com

GATHER SOME GLASS ART
AT GATHERED GLASS

Toledo is home to the studio glass movement. Today, several excellent glass studios are practicing the technique first developed in a garage on the Toledo Museum of Art campus in 1962. Gathered Glass is one of those studios specializing in handmade functional glass objects for everyday pleasure, custom site-specific glass installations, and private and group glassblowing workshops. Recently, a business colleague who was in town for a snowy winter weekend enjoyed creating her first glass masterpiece, a custom Christmas ornament, with the help of the instructors at Gathered Glass.

Located in the heart of the Warehouse District, the studio is surrounded by new development, nightlife, and other creative businesses. They also lease artist studio space to local artists and artisans.

23 N Huron St., (419) 262-5501, gatheredglass.com

● ●

TIP

Looking for more places to shop for beautiful glass in the Glass City? Here are a few more recommendations:

Firenation Glass Studio and Gallery
A prolific studio offering a variety of glass art, classes, and workshops.
7166 Front St., Holland, firenation.com

The Glass Pavilion
Incredible displays of historic glass items, glassblowing demonstrations, and classes.
2444 Monroe St., toledomuseum.org/about/glass-tma

Schmidt Messenger Studios
Small, private studio.
340 Morris St., artfulhome.com/artist/
Shawn-E-Messenger/7944

SPREAD YOUR WINGS
AT ANGELWOOD GALLERY

Established in 1993, Angelwood Gallery is one of the oldest privately owned galleries in northwest Ohio. Angelwood features the artwork of Julie Beutler, the owner and potter, specializing in functional stoneware. She is an award-winning artist with her work in private collections all around the world. The gallery also showcases glass, wood, painting, metal, jewelry, and photography from many other artists, mostly from Ohio and Michigan.

Angelwood Gallery is the ideal place to find unique gifts to decorate your home or office or add that perfect piece to your collection. The gallery features several shows throughout the year with new artwork added each month. This is a great place to peruse incredible art any time of the year.

24195 Front St., Grand Rapids, (419) 832-0625
angelwoodgallery.com

GET YOUR GARDEN FIX
AT TITGEMEIER'S FEED AND GARDEN

A south Toledo landmark, Titgemeier's has had the same location since it was established more than a century ago and has been in the same family for four generations! Well known as the "most unusual store" that urges shoppers to "take a bird to lunch," their products range from lawn and garden supplies to pet supplies to beer and winemaking products.

Nestled in a predominately German immigrant neighborhood on Toledo's outskirts, Fred Titgemeier opened the feed and flour store in a wooden house on Western Avenue and Marion Street in 1888. The store still sells some chicken feed and straw, but today, it's brewing and vinting supplies that carry the business through winter, while grass seed and fertilizer are big in the summer. The store also sells garden tools and supplies, a variety of seeds for wild birds, and an array of pet goods. This is an unusual store you need to put on your list of places to visit in Toledo.

701 Western Ave., (419) 243-3731, titgemeiers.com

Photo courtesy of Tedd Long

SUGGESTED
ITINERARIES

FOR ART LOVERS

Admire World-Class Fine Art at the Toledo Museum of Art, 72

Tour the Art Loop, 84

Expand Your Horizons at 20 North Gallery, 119

Gather Some Glass Art at Gathered Glass, 126

Experience the Sheer Beauty of Our Lady, Queen of the
Most Holy Rosary Cathedral, 93

Buy a Masterpiece at the Crosby Arts Festival, 104

Spread Your Wings at Angelwood Gallery, 128

FOR THE FAMILY

Power Your Kids' Dreams at Imagination Station, 77

Delight in a World-Famous Hungarian Hot Dog at Tony Packo's, 2

See More Than 1,000 Butterflies at the Butterfly House, 78

Adore Music Under the Stars at the Toledo Zoo Amphitheater, 44

Get a Kick Out of Life at Pacesetter Park's Soccer Fields, 64

Sleep in a Tree at the Metroparks Cannaley Treehouse Village, 98

Hit the Books at Main Library, 96

FOR DATE NIGHT

FOR HISTORY BUFFS

FOR OUTDOOR LOVERS

• •

ACTIVITIES
BY SEASON

SPRING

Fish the Walleye Run on the Maumee River, 65

Play the First Public Golf Course West of New York at Ottawa Park, 60

Get a Kick Out of Life at Pacesetter Park's Soccer Fields, 64

Take a Walk in Victorian and Edwardian Splendor in the Old West End, 74

See More Than 1,000 Butterflies at the Butterfly House, 78

Take in a Spectacular Sunset at Grand Rapids, 112

SUMMER

Buy a Masterpiece at the Crosby Arts Festival, 104

Celebrate East Toledo's Hungarian Culture at the Birmingham Festival, 88

Lap Up Food, Drink, and Dance at the German American Festival, 89

Holler "Opa" at the Greek American Festival, 90

Revel in Family Fun at the Toledo African American Parade and Festival, 91

Chase the Blues Away at Griffin Hines Farms, 49

Hit a Home Run with the Toledo Mud Hens, 54

Watch 'em Trade Paint at Toledo Speedway, 55

Catch Your Limit of Perch on Lake Erie with the West Sister Charter Fleet, 67

• •

FALL

WINTER

• •

Photo courtesy of Tedd Long

INDEX

• •

Photo courtesy of Tedd Long